MR J.
2 DOWLII
SNOI
KENT. I

BRIGHT

THE RETURN OF THE NATIVE BY THOMAS HARDY

Intelligent Education

INFLUENCE PUBLISHERS

Nashville, Tennessee

BRIGHT NOTES: The Return of the Native
www.BrightNotes.com

No part of this publication may be used or reproduced in any manner whatsoever without written permission, except in the case of brief quotations in critical articles and reviews. For permissions, contact Influence Publishers http://www.influencepublishers.com.

ISBN: 978-1-645424-92-5 (Paperback)
ISBN: 978-1-645424-93-2 (eBook)

Published in accordance with the U.S. Copyright Office Orphan Works and Mass Digitization report of the register of copyrights, June 2015.

Originally published by Monarch Press.
Charles L. Leavitt; Emily S. Leavitt, 1964
2019 Edition published by Influence Publishers.

Interior design by Lapiz Digital Services. Cover Design by Thinkpen Designs.

Printed in the United States of America.

Library of Congress Cataloging-in-Publication Data forthcoming.
Names: Intelligent Education
Title: BRIGHT NOTES: The Return of the Native
Subject: STU004000 STUDY AIDS / Book Notes

CONTENTS

INTRODUCTION TO THOMAS HARDY

. . . .

HARDY'S BIRTH AND PARENTAGE

Thomas Hardy was born in Upper Bockhampton, Dorsetshire, England, on June 2, 1840. His father was known then as a master builder (today we would call him a contractor) who employed up to ten or twelve men on his buildings. Hardy's mother came of a family long established in Dorset as cultivators of the land. Ernest Brennecke in his *Life of Thomas Hardy* says she was ambitious in a literary way; her interests included the classical Latin poets, Virgil, French romances and tragedies. From her Hardy developed his love of reading. It was she who arranged what formal education Hardy received: first the village school; then her own tutoring in Latin; then a French governess for a year. Thereafter Hardy was his own tutor, teaching himself Greek, and reading eagerly and thoughtfully.

YOUTH

In 1856 Hardy, ages sixteen, was apprenticed to a Dorchester architect, whom he helped in the restoration of old churches. In 1862, at twenty-two, he went to London to work in another architect's office. He won a prize for an essay, "The Application of Coloured Bricks and Terra Cotta in Modern Architecture."

During his time in London Hardy attended night classes offered by King's College. In his spare time he wrote poetry. He spent much time at concerts and in the art museums. Hardy endured London for five years before he returned to Dorset in 1867 to work for the same architect who had apprenticed him.

LATER YEARS

Through his work on restoring a church in Cornwall, Hardy met the church organist, Emma Lavinia Gifford, whom he married in 1874. During their early married years, after a honeymoon in Paris and Belgium, they lived in Dorset, London, and at times in a Paris flat. Although her preferred writing poetry, he turned to writing novels as a means of earning money. His novels were first published in installments in popular magazines. Between 1883 and 1885 he built, near Dorchester, his own home which he called Max Gate. In 1912 the first Mrs. rarely moved from his beloved Wessex country. In 1912 the first Mrs. Hardy died. In 1914 Hardy married his secretary, Florence Emily Dugdale. She was a writer herself, and after Hardy's death, in 1928, she devoted her time to assembling his biography from his papers and her own reminiscences. Her *Life of Thomas Hardy* was first published in 1933.

HARDY'S PERSONALITY

Albert Guerard, a noted critic, speaks of Hardy as having the tenderness of a Saint Francis toward children, animals, and all unfortunates, Katherine Anne Porter, in an essay in *Modern Literary Criticism*, says that Hardy was painfully sensitive to what he believed to be a universal pervasiveness of needless misery for humans and animals. All his life he suffered underlying selfless discomfort for the suffering of all animate beings. H. M. Tomlinson, in an essay in *The Saturday Review Gallery*, believes that the only thing that could arouse Hardy's anger was cruelty to humble and insignificant people or to animals. His greatness lay in simple, modest thoughts and concerns. He liked to talk of nature, the birds and the signs of the weather; he liked to ramble on about the village inns and the characters who frequented them. The little things of life interested him for he was a man of simple tastes and habits.

LITERARY CAREER

At the outset of his book on Hardy, Henry Duffin gives a chronology and classification of Hardy's literary works. Hardy began writing as a poet and ended writing as a poet. Poetry was his favorite means of expression; but writing poetry did not provide a livelihood; so he turned to writing popular novels.

Hardy wrote fourteen Wessex novels between 1871 and 1895. *The Return of the Native* (1878) is the sixth of those novels. Hardy classified his fiction as: Novels of Character and Environment; Romances and Fantasies; Novels of Ingenuity and Experiment. *The Return of the Native* he called a Novel of Character and Environment. Mr. Duffin suggests another classification - Tragedies, Tragi-comedies, Comedies - and lists *The Return of the Native* as a Tragedy.

The last of the Wessex novels, *Jude the Obscure*, published in 1895, created such a furor in ecclesiastical circles that Hardy, a devout churchman, gave up writing novels and returned to his first love, poetry. The dates of the poetry volumes range from 1898 to his death in 1928.

Critics differ as to which of Hardy's novels is his greatest: *The Return of the Native*, *Tess of the D'Urbervilles*, or *Jude the Obscure*. From the number of editions of *The Return of the Native* now published, it seems that this novel is the most popular at the present time.

WESSEX COUNTRY

Historically, Wessex was one of the kingdoms of Anglo-Saxon Britain. Geographically, it first included what are now the counties of Dorset, Somerset, and Devon; later it annexed what are now Surrey, Kent, Sussex, and Essex. The Wessex of Hardy's novels encompasses Dorsetshire, Hampshire, and Wiltshire. On the map it describes a semi-circle southward with Oxford as the northernmost point.

Ernest Brennecke, in his biography, says that Hardy looked upon the heath country of Wessex as if it were a great stage upon which nature buffeted the animate and inanimate about in comedies and tragedies dependent upon the sum of all the long past actions of history as well as upon the present unpredictable moods of weather and vast solitude. Albert Guerard enumerates the important Wessex virtues as fidelity, simplicity, endurance, and tolerance. Wessex contains heath country unchanged over the centuries since the Romans buried their dead in the huge earthworks now known as barrows. Guerard calls Hardy the Wessex historian and further notes that Hardy's rural characters are really not of the nineteenth century, but are characters out of Wessex history which they help to keep alive.

In his childhood, Hardy made his playground on the heath; his playmates were heath children. He learned early to talk the heath dialect, although in his home he was not allowed to use it. That his heart and soul were firmly attached to the Wessex country is shown by Max Gate, the home he built on the edge of the heath and rarely left. H. M. Tomlinson visited Hardy at Max Gate and writes of the place in an essay. Max Gate, near Dorchester, is like an island walled by trees from the vast expanse of Egdon Heath. The house is completely hidden from the road. Hardy probably planted the screen of trees to protect his cherished privacy. One could walk across the fields from the town and feel the dark mood of the brooding hill beyond fields of corn. Maiden Castle, an ancient Celtic earthwork or hillfort formed by men long before the Romans came, rises in the distance. Dorchester church with its square tower, and the chimneys of the town seem to float over the treetops which rise from the depression below the height of the town. This is real Hardy country, and you feel you must be about to meet the man himself, no matter which path you take.

THE RETURN OF THE NATIVE

Hardy classified this work as a Novel of Character and Environment. Albert Guerard calls it a tragedy of cross purpose, which is universal and vast. Here we have the brooding heath, less concerned over human beings caught in its spell than human beings are concerned over the plight of ants in an anthill on its wild surface. Here we have characters, themselves strong personalities, playing upon each other and played upon by this imperturbable environment. Guerard says that Hardy believed literally in the power of imagination over the body and in the magnetic, compelling power of the strong mind over the weak. In *The Return of the Native* the heath is the ultimate strong mind.

THE STORY IN BRIEF

Eustacia Vye, a nineteen-year-old, sultry beauty, has one compelling desire: to marry a man worthy of her and to travel to exotic distant lands with him as her cavalier. Living on Egdon Heath, she has only one possible candidate: Damon Wildeve, keeper of the village inn, a former civil engineer who somehow failed in his profession. Wildeve and Eustacia Vye have equally uncurbed passionate natures. They seem to thrive on tormenting each other - now passionately loving, now passionately hating. Wildeve, however, has a roving eye which has been caught by the innocent simplicity of Thomasin Yeobright. She is not one to be trifled with, and he has asked her to marry him; but at church on the wedding day, whether by his intent, or by his mistake, the license proves invalid. Eustacia is overjoyed at the news, thinking Wildeve is so much in love with her that he cannot marry another.

Thomasin Yeobright, however, has a protector, Diggory Venn. Diggory is in love with Thomasin. He has earlier proposed to her but has been gently refused. Diggory determines that she shall have the man she wants. He and Mrs. Yeobright, Thomasin's aunt, contrive separately and together, to bring about the delayed wedding.

Eustacia, confronted with an actual proposal of marriage from Wildeve, cannot bring herself to believe him good enough for her; neither can she bring herself to accept what she considers second place, since Thomasin received his first proposal of marriage.

The arrival of Clym Yeobright, Mrs. Yeobright's son, stirs Eustacia's spirit of adventure. Clym's business is in Paris. Bright lights glitter in Eustacia's mind. Clym is well-educated and well-to-do; he is her knight-in-armor come to rescue her; Thomasin, his earlier sweetheart, must not get him. Eustacia joins the schemers to bring about the postponed wedding of Thomasin and Damon Wildeve. Meanwhile Mrs. Yeobright, by telling Wildeve of another suitor who wants Thomasin, rekindles his desire for her. Diggory Venn, by admitting himself the other suitor, and Eustacia Vye, by spurning Wildeve's proposal to her, send Wildeve, in a pique, to set a date with Thomasin.

Thomasin marries Wildeve. Wildeve thinks he is having revenge on Eustacia, but Eustacia is happy to have Thomasin removed as a rival for Clym Yeobright's affections. When Clym marries Eustacia, despite his mother's disapproval of the "hussy," he has to move from his mother's house because of the rift, and the wedding is without her blessing or presence.

Eustacia has heard Clym say that he wants to stay on the health and become a teacher, but she cannot believe that anyone who has been to Paris will not go back there. By the end of their honeymoon, however, she realizes his firm resolve never to go back. Clym plunges deeper into his studies to hasten his becoming a teacher, and thus ruins his eyesight. Unable to read for months, he finds in furze-cutting (cutting bushes on the heath) an occupation which enables him to keep his self-respect. Eustacia, however, is humiliated and in despair.

Clym's mother, learning of his misfortune through Diggory Venn (the ever-watchful one), is persuaded to relent and go to call on the couple. Through a mistake, however, no one answers her knocks, though she knows her son, his wife, and another man are in the house. She stumbles back over the heath in the broiling sun, to be found later by her son in a state of exhaustion from which she dies.

Clym is ill and broken-hearted for weeks. He cannot understand how his mother could have been turned from his door thinking she was cast off by her son, as a neighbor boy reports. He blindly blames himself and will not be comforted. Finally he learns that it all happened while he was taking his mid-day nap. Eustacia has a visitor with her and, thinking Clym had roused to answer his mother's knock, had not gone to the door. Clym demands to know who the visitor was. Eustacia will not say. Clym, beside himself with rage and grief, says things that drive Eustacia from the cottage back to her grandfather's house at Mistover.

Eustacia meets secretly with Wildeve, who has now inherited a considerable sum of money. He agrees to help Eustacia escape to the seaport, inwardly planning to escape with her. She still has her dream of Paris; he relishes the thought of an illicit elopement with her.

Thomasin suspects the plan and goes to Clym, her cousin, for help. He sets forth to intercept the pair; Thomasin goes on to ask help of Diggory Venn. Diggory and Thomasin go together to the place where Clym and Wildeve have met - on the heath road beside the river. Suddenly they all hear a dull thud and soon discover that Eustacia, overwhelmed by the futility of it all, has slipped or flung herself into the water to drown. Wildeve and Clym Yeobright both swim to rescue her. All three are finally dragged from the water by Diggory Venn. Eustacia and Wildeve are dead, but Clym is revived.

Hardy's sixth book of the novel, written at the demand of his public, has Thomasin, now a widow, marry her faithful lover, Diggory Venn. Clym Yeobright plunges on alone through life in his chosen professions of teaching and preaching.

THE RETURN OF THE NATIVE

TEXTUAL ANALYSIS

BOOK FIRST: THE THREE WOMEN

. . . .

CHAPTER 1: A FACE ON WHICH TIME MAKES BUT LITTLE IMPRESSION

The time is November - a Saturday afternoon approaching twilight. The place is Egdon Heath, covered by a sky completely overcast. Imagine being in a vast rounded tent made of clouds with the heath as the floor. The dark brown heath and the whitish sky make it seem that night has come while day still lingers. "Looking upwards, a furze-cutter [furze is an evergreen shrub] would have been inclined to continue work; looking down, he would have decided to finish his faggot [bundle] and go home." Thus the dark face of the heath could "hasten evening," "intensify midnight," "retard dawn," and "sadden noon." The approach of night seems to bring the heath to life. Darkness becomes a living, pulsing being, exhaled by the heath to meet the waning light from the heavens. As all else sinks to sleep, the heath awakens and becomes an intent listener. It seems to be waiting, "a lonely face, suggesting tragical possibilities," friend to the wind, beloved of the storm. Twilight combines with "the scenery of Egdon Heath to evolve a thing majestic ... impressive ... emphatic ... grand": a "sublimity" or appeal to the soul, often lacking in places famous for scenic beauty.

The human soul has suffered oftener from a place too smiling for its reason than from oppressive surroundings "oversadly tinged." As our race has advanced in years, the more thinking among mankind have found "closer harmony with external things wearing a sombreness": "the chastened sublimity of a moor, a sea, or a mountain" - or "a gaunt waste in Thule." Egdon Heath answers to this call from the spirit of man. Its intensity is the sort "arrived at during winter darkness, tempests, and mists." It invites the illusion of strange phantoms - the wild regions which harass "in midnight dreams of flight and disaster."

History, recording in the *Domesday Book* (record of old English landowners) the length and breadth of this wilderness, shows that the area of Egdon has not diminished. Mention of the right of heath-turf cutting occurs in the early charters of the district, but any changes in the land have not been made "by pickaxe, plow, or spade." They remain as "finger-touches of the last geological change." Here the scene is set: on the brown heath breathing darkness toward the twilight sky. The light of the sky in its turn serves to mark out the sole brightness of the land - a sandy road winding like a thread along the lower hollows between rounds and rises from one horizon to the other.

Comment

This chapter sets the tone for the whole book. We are introduced to Egdon Heath, the center of all the action. To Hardy, Egdon Heath is much more than a place; it is a living being responding to the whims of nature; it is a mood, casting a spell over all who know it. Hardy casts its spell over us. He uses "November" and "Saturday afternoon" and "twilight" to establish a somber, darkening mood. He uses the shifting clouds in the sky as contrasts, to add stormy motion to the mood. He is telling us that this is to be a story of strong emotions, midnight calamities, mysterious events; a story of the people of the heath country and how they are affected by this environment. Egdon Heath will have a powerful effect on the characters of the story, moving them to love or to hate, to despair or to resignation. Egdon Heath holds the threads of a grim and tragic tapestry - the separate, lonely lives of its people. With the mood well set, Hardy reveals to us the first tangible link of the heath with humanity - the road.

CHAPTER 2: HUMANITY APPEARS UPON THE SCENE, HAND IN HAND WITH TROUBLE

Along the road walks an old man. He seems from his ancient and faded garb to have been a naval officer of some sort. He stabs into the ground with a silver-headed walking stick at equal intervals with the stomping of his sturdy legs. Before him stretches "the long, laborious road" bisecting the dark surface of the heath "like the parting line on a head of black hair." Stretching his eyes ahead of him, the old man sees, far beyond, a moving spot. Although it is advancing away from him, its pace is slower than his own. As the traveler draws near, he discovers the spot to be a "spring van of a lurid red color." The driver walking beside it is also completely red. "One dye of that tincture" covers "his clothes, the cap upon his head, his boots, his face, his hands." He is not just "temporarily overlaid with the color"; he is permeated with it. The old man knows him for a reddleman, "a person whose vocation" it is to "supply farmers with redding for their sheep." As the ancient navy man comes alongside, he calls out a greeting to which the reddleman replies "in sad and occupied tones."

He is a young man whose smooth-shaven face is probably handsome in its natural color. His blue eyes are keen as a hawk's. His suit of corduroy is of excellent quality and well chosen for his work. He carries himself with a well-to-do air. One would wonder: "Why should such a promising being as this have hidden his prepossessing exterior by adopting that singular occupation?" The two travelers walk side by side without speaking further, hearing only the sounds of the heath. At short intervals the reddleman leaves his companion and, stepping behind, peers into a small window of the van. Each time he returns the older man ventures a remark or two to which the younger man replies absent-mindedly. They lapse into silence and plod on for miles without talking.

After the fifth of the reddleman's visits to the van, his walking companion begins to question him. He learns that there is a young woman sleeping uneasily inside the wagon. She has been riding thus from Anglebury and is being taken home. The old man grows bolder in his questioning, but the reddleman refuses to divulge anything more. He explains that his ponies are tired. "I am going to rest them under this bank for an hour." So the old traveler proceeds on his way.

The reddleman watches the advancing figure gradually become absorbed "in the thickening films of night." He then takes down some hay for the ponies and, settling himself on a pad, musingly surveys the scene around him. This scene is "a gradual series of ascents from the level of the road backward into the heart of the heath." It embraces "hillocks, pits, ridges, acclivities one behind the other… finished by a high hill cutting against the still light sky." As the young man's eyes scan the heights along the skyline, they settle "upon one noteworthy object… a barrow. This bossy projection of earth above its natural level" occupies the "loftiest ground of the loneliest height" that the heath contains. From the vale it appears "as a wart on an Atlantean brow," but "its actual bulk is great." It forms the "pole and axis of this heathery world." As the reddleman watches, he sees the barrow "surmounted by something higher," rising "like a spike from a helmet." To the young man in the valley, the scene is viewed in waves: "Above the plain ... the hill, above the hill ... the barrow, and above the barrow ... the figure." Above and around the figure is the sky. Suddenly the figure shifts, turns around and, descending "with the glide of a water-drop down a bud," vanishes from sight. The movements are sufficient to reveal the disappearing form to be that of a woman. The reason for her departure soon becomes evident; one form after another appears, each bearing a burden to be deposited on top, until finally "the whole barrow is peopled with burdened figures."

Comment

The road immediately brings us into contact with our first human being. The old man on the road leads us to the mysterious van (a little house on wheels drawn by two ponies) and the mysterious reddleman (one who deals in reddle, which is red ocher or red chalk for marking sheep). In the wagon is the mysterious sleeping woman. By the reddleman's concern for her, we believe her to be an important character. Hardy is very slowly unraveling the thread of his tale. The reddleman is an odd creature to us, but we find him likable. We feel he will be one of the likable characters. When the traveler goes on alone, the reddleman settles down to survey the darkening scene around him. We get a stronger, higher impression of the heath. We look up to the top of a large barrow (a mound of earth or stones built over graves by the Celts, early settlers of England) and see a solitary figure outlined against the sky. The figure disappears. The barrow now swarms with people; but we are given the impression that the one person who preceded them," the lonely person who ... had been queen of the solitude," is to be an important character in the story-possibly a mysterious one. Hardy is showing himself a master artist in building suspense. We know no names but Egdon Heath; we feel a mood of "calm before a storm," an ominous foreboding; we now know of four individuals, two men and two women, but we have no names for them.

CHAPTER 3: THE CUSTOM OF THE COUNTRY

The "burdened figures" swarming over the top of Rainbarrow are men and boys, each carrying on his shoulder a long pole sharpened at both ends and strung with furze-faggots. The effect is as if an acre of bushes has sprouted legs and is invading the barrow-top. As the men deposit their burdens, the furze-faggots are loosened, spread, and piled into a pyramid thirty feet around. Matches light the driest tufts, and a huge bonfire blazes up into the sky. Almost immediately similar fires burst out all over the expanse of the heath as far as an eye can see. As this fire burns, we become conscious of the country folk as individuals. (Women and children have now reached the top to join their men.) The oldest man, Grandfer Cantle, begins to jig and sing "in the voice of a bee up a flue." Someone, calling attention to "a dim light in the direction of the distant highway" asks, "And how about the new-married folks down there at the Quiet Woman Inn?"

The question starts a flurry of village gossip. We learn of Mrs. Yeobright, the young bride's aunt: that her son Clym is expected home to keep her company now her niece has left her; that she had at first forbidden the banns but has since "come around." The bride's name is revealed to be Thomasin Yeobright.

Her husband, Damon Wildeve, an engineer by profession, "threw away his chance" and is now keeper of the village inn. The couple (they think) has been married this very afternoon. Some complain because the wedding did not take place in the village where they could all make a merry celebration. The men plot to give "the new man and wife a bit of a song tonight... when the womenfolk and youngsters have gone home.... Strike up a ballet in front of the married folks' door." There is talk of ghosts. Timothy Fairway speaks of a strange one that has been seen lately: "A red one. Yes, most ghosts be white; but this is as if it had been dipped in blood." The big bonfire and the other fires over the heath begin to flicker out - all except one, which is the nearest of any to Rainbarrow. "It lay in a direction precisely opposite to that of the little window" at the Quiet Woman-Inn. Comment about it puts it at about a mile and a half off, near Captain Vye's house of Mistover Knap. Some guess that it is being kept by his granddaughter, since "Cap'n Vye has been for a long walk today and is quite tired out." The dying embers of the Rainbarrow fire give an eerie light. As a last jolly spurt, Timothy Fairway seizes Susan Nunsuch round the waist and whirls her off to "the site of the fire ... now merely a circle of ashes flecked with red embers and sparks .... Once within the circle he whirled her round and round in a dance .... The turfcutter seized old Olly Dowden .... The young men ... seized the maids; Grandfer Cantle and his stick jigged in the form of a three-legged object among the rest.... The chief noises were women's shrill cries, men's laughter, Susan's stays and pattens, Olly Dowden's ('heu-heu-heu!') and the strumming of the wind upon the furze-bushes."

They are all startled to a standstill by a voice from the darkness: "Hoi-i-i-i!" Fairway answers with a "Halloo-o-o-o." As the stranger approaches, the men light a few stray bits of furze to see his face. It is the reddleman. He inquires if there is a wagon track across to Mrs. Yeobright's house. They give him directions, and with thanks, he starts back to his van which is "in the bottom, about half a mile back." Hardly has he disappeared, when another person appears. "Why, 'tis Mis'ess Yeo-bright," says Timothy Fairway in recognition, and he tells her a reddleman has just been asking for her. Mrs. Yeobright explains that she is crossing the heath to her niece's new home and came up hoping that Olly Dowden would "walk with me, as her way is mine." Olly agrees and points out the "light shining from your niece's window.... It will help us keep the path." The two women start on their way together, leaving the others to take a rougher short-cut through the furze-bushes.

Comment

Here we are given a vivid country picture of the English custom of celebrating Guy Fawkes Day. (Guy Fawkes was the "fall guy" in the famous "Gunpowder Plot" against Parliament in 1605. The plot was organized by Roman Catholics against James I and his Parliament who were reviving anti-Roman Catholic laws. A ton of gunpowder was concealed in the basement of the House of Lords. This was to be set off by Guy Fawkes on November fifth when Parliament was in session. The plot was discovered and Guy Fawkes was executed. Present day Englishmen celebrate November fifth with bonfires or fireworks.) Hardy uses this special fall celebration to introduce us to the humble folk of the heath in their jolliest mood. Through them we hear gossip about the novel's major characters. Hardy has a masterly way of building up his main characters bit by bit. In this chapter, they are not "on stage," but we learn a lot about them and the events which have led up to the present. In addition, we find ourselves acquainted with loveable country folk: Grandfer Cantle with his jigs and jokes; his simple son, Christian, who touches us with his frantic fears; plump Susan Nunsuch "whose stays creak like shoes"; Olly Dowden, the humble broom maker; Timothy Fairway, the general leader of the villagers. By the speeches he gives to each. Hardy makes these people alive personalities for us, like people we have known.

CHAPTER 4: THE HALT ON THE TURNPIKE ROAD

As the two women descend Rainbarrow, Olly chats in her simple manner with Mrs. Yeobright. She speaks of the marriage and of Mrs. Yeobright's opposition to it, saying, "I felt myself that he was hardly solid-going enough to mate with your family," though "he've several acres of heath ground broke up here, besides the public house, and the heth-croppers, and his manners be quite like a gentleman's." Mrs. Yeobright agrees with Olly that "what's done cannot be undone." They reach the wagon track. Olly turns toward her own home, calling out to her companion to remind Wildeve of the bottle of wine he has promised her sick husband on the occasion of his marriage. Mrs. Yeobright follows the track to the highway. As she approaches the Inn, she notices a horse-drawn wagon coming along the highway, a man walking beside it, lantern in hand. She waits to speak: "I think you have been inquiring for me? I am Mrs. Yeobright of Blooms-End." The reddlemen motions for silence. He draws her aside and is recognized by her as "young Venn - your father was a dairyman somewhere here?" He tells how her niece caught up with him and asked to ride home in his van. He then assists Mrs. Yeobright into the wagon where, under the lantern's rays, she sees her niece sleeping, carefully protected from the reddle by drapery. Thomasin awakens; the reddleman tactfully moves outside to the front of the wagon, so that aunt and niece may talk. Upon finding out where she is, Thomasin desires to walk on home from there. Thanking Diggory Venn for his kindness, Mrs. Yeobright asks, "What made you change from the nice business your father left you?" He looks briefly at Thomasin, who blushes a little, and replies merely, "Well, I did." He starts his horses onward and the two women are left alone. "Now, Thomasin," says Mrs. Yeobright sternly, "what's the meaning of this disgraceful performance?"

Comment

Hardy here displays two women for contrast. Olly Dowden, the humble broom maker, is used to highlight Mrs. Yeobright's gentility and strength of spirit. The certain imperiousness in Mrs. Yeobright's manner to Olly makes us feel she is a woman to be reckoned with. Diggory Venn is further shown to be a kindly, considerate person through his tactful manner with Thomasin and her aunt.

CHAPTER 5: PERPLEXITY AMONG HONEST PEOPLE

Thomasin tells her aunt that she is not married. Because of some irregularity in the license, the parson would not perform the ceremony. She had felt so humiliated that she ran away from her intended husband and, overtaking Diggory Venn, begged a ride home in his van. Mrs. Yeobright insists that they go into the Inn to confront Wildeve and hear his side of the story. Wildeve greets Thomasin with careless affection. He explains that the license had been made out for Budmouth and the pastor at Anglebury would not honor it. Thomasin begs to speak with him alone, and they go into an adjoining room, where Thomasin apologizes for her behavior. She asks him if he means to marry her. He enjoys dangling the decision for a while to tantalize her, but finally, carelessly, agrees.

Just then, singing voices are heard outside. The men and boys have come to serenade the married couple. Mrs. Yeobright joins Thomasin in the back room while Wildeve goes to the door. He invites the men in for refreshment, and under the mellowing influence of the mead, the men reminisce among themselves about the fine musician Thomasin's father had been, and now he had died unexpectedly in early life. As they all get ready to leave, Timothy Fairway notes through the window the small bonfire still burning steadily over the heath at Captain Vye's. The simple Christian Cantle suggests, "Perhaps there's meaning in it." Wildeve turns on him sharply and asks how, but "Christian is too scattered to reply." Others mention that Captain Vye's granddaughter has been called a witch by some, but they all agree she is a handsome young woman. Wildeve goes out to see the singers off. Upon his return to the back room, he finds that the women have left by the window. Amused, he returns to the front room and, noticing a bottle of wine standing on the mantelpiece, starts off down the road with it tucked under his arm. (He remembers his promise to Olly Dowden's sick husband.) As he walks, however, he sees the bonfire winking at him. Olly's house has only a faint light in the upstairs window, so he enters the dark downstairs room and leaves the bottle on the table. Back outside again on the heath, he finds he must heed the bonfire's summons and "go to her."

Comment

Hardy, in one deft sentence, reveals Mrs. Yeobright's two-sided character: "I could almost say it serves you right-if I did not feel that you don't deserve it," is her first reaction to her niece's story. We smile at the contradiction and the human spirit of the woman. By dialogue (Thomasin with her aunt, Thomasin with Wildeve) Thomasin's character is now sketched into place. We see she is a gentle-spirited, romantic young girl, with a certain dogged determination. She has some amount of pride and a dignity that controls her emotions. She has a protective instinct toward those she loves. "I've not let aunt know how much I have suffered today: and it is so hard to command my face and voice, and to smile as if it were a slight thing to me; but I try to do so, that she may not be still more indignant with you." Thus she speaks to Wildeve. By his replies we recognize Wildeve as a lady killer, who toys with women's affections. He is "one in whom no man would have seen anything to admire, and in whom no woman would have seen anything to dislike." He also is proud, and his pride has been cut. He feels compelled to marry Thomasin to get even with her aunt for her public insult to him. Hardy again uses villagers' gossip (when the men come for merry-making) to tell us bits about the major characters.

CHAPTER 6: THE FIGURE AGAINST THE SKY

Now we are to find out about the figure that rose from Rainbarrow "like a spike from a helmet" when the reddleman first surveyed Egdon Heath. As soon as everyone has left the top of Rainbarrow, this same figure, closely wrapped, climbs to the summit again. She approaches from the place where the little fire is still burning. Reaching the top, she stands still for some moments, listening to the sounds of the heath. Noticing the light at the Quiet Woman Inn, she takes out a telescope and gazes at the Inn. Finally, closing the telescope, she stoops to blow on a live coal. The light flares up, revealing an hourglass-with all the sand slipped through to the lower half. With a slight exclamation she picks it up, and with the telescope under her arm walks on down a faint path leading toward the still burning fire. As she approaches the fire, which is on a bank near a pool, she can see a small hand putting on fuel. "Occasionally an ember rolled off the bank, and dropped with a hiss into the pool." The young woman walks to the bonfire, and is greeted by a little boy: "I am glad you have come, Miss Eustacia.... I don't like biding by myself."

From the conversation we learn that Eustacia Vye has been pacing back and forth from her bonfire over various parts of the heath all evening. Her grandfather comes out to urge her to come inside, but she excuses herself, insisting that Johnny wants the fire a little longer. Johnny is not so sure he does, but Eustacia speaks to him sharply, bending his will to hers. The grandfather goes back to the house. Eustacia promises Johnny "a crooked sixpence" if he will keep putting wood on the fire, "And if you hear a frog jump into the pond ... like a stone thrown in, be sure you run and tell me, because it is a sign of rain." Eustacia keeps wandering off and coming back at intervals. Finally Johnny slides down the bank to run to tell her, "A hop frog have jumped into the pond. Yes, I heard 'en!" Eustacia gives him the crooked sixpence, telling him to run off home fast. When he has gone, she walks toward an angle of the bank under the fire. She hears another splash and steps out upon the bank. The man, Wildeve, comes round the bank and leaps up beside her. Eustacia gives a low laugh of triumph. Her power over him has again drawn him to her. When he asks why she gives him no peace, she insists the bonfire is just for celebration; but he reminds her that last year it was a signal. She confesses that it is so tonight. They talk in passionate tones, now admitting their power over each other, now denying it. She tells Wildeve the signal is because she believes him to be faithful to her by not marrying Thomasin; he asks how she is so sure he is not married.

She is deeply offended to find he believes she sent the signal thinking him married. In a pout she tells him to go home, refusing even to let him take her hand, and "with the bow of a dancing master" he vanishes. After scattering the burning embers, Eustacia goes inside, undressing in the dark, heaving great sighs that shake her whole being.

Comment

In this chapter Hardy shows us Eustacia Vye's personality through her actions: she is imperious in her manner with little Johnny and her father; she is capricious with her lover, now leading him on, now thrusting him away. Men to her are beings to be molded to her will. She is revealed as a creature ruled by a compelling, passionate nature, and as her own worst enemy. She and Wildeve are much alike: unscrupulous in plotting; wanting something only if it is hard to get; losing interest in anything easily attained.

CHAPTER 7: QUEEN OF THE NIGHT

Eustacia Vye is "the raw material of a goddess." With "the new moon behind her head" and "an old helmet upon it" she resembles the Greek goddess Athena. Her long thick hair has the blackness of night. Her strong temper can always be softened by brushing her hair. Her eyes are languid, with oppressive lids and lashes, making her seem to be in a reverie. Her soul might be said to be the color of flame. "Celestial imperiousness" and "smoldering rebelliousness" combine to make her a woman of caprice. She was born in Budmouth, a fashionable seaside town. Her father, a native of Corfu, was a bandmaster and a fine musician, while her mother was of a good English family. Her girlhood memories are of "sunny afternoons on an esplanade, with military bands, officers, and gallants around."

After the death of her father and mother, Eustacia has come with her grandfather to live on Egdon Heath. "To be loved to madness" is her great desire - a longing for passionate love consumes her soul. But here on the heath, far from the glitter of the town, she has come to feel that nothing is worthwhile.

She idealizes Wildeve because there is no better man available. She herself knows this, and at times she rebels against her passion. Her spirits are depressed, but she often takes long walks on the heath, carrying her "grandfather's telescope and her grandmother's hourglass". When she decides to scheme she can use the strategy of a general.

Comment

Hardy now paints in words a portrait of Eustacia Vye. Her passionate, fiery nature she inherits from her father, who was a native of Corfu - that island, west of Greece, where Italians and Greeks have bred a people of fiery Latin temperament. Eustacia's great pride is inherited from her mother, who is indicated as a woman of middle-class, snobbish gentility. Swayed by great passion and by great pride, Eustacia is a victim of moods and whims. She pursues a man ruthlessly, only to cast him off when he becomes her slave. Perhaps Hardy's most famous description of her comes in these lines: "The only way to look queenly without realms or hearts to queen it over is to look as if you had lost them." Proud, she scorns anything easily attainable or common to others. "She only valued rest to herself when it came in the midst of other people's labor." She can hardly be happy unless others are unhappy.

CHAPTER 8: THOSE WHO ARE FOUND WHERE THERE IS SAID TO BE NOBODY

Little Johnny, after leaving Eustacia Vye's bonfire, has about three-eighths of a mile to go home. First he runs till he is out of breath; then, slowing down, he walks along at an easy pace, singing a song, and clutching his sixpence to give him courage.

Suddenly, ahead of him, he sees a dusty light and hears a slapping noise. He turns back, frightened, thinking to ask Miss Eustacia to have her servant go home with him; but finding that Eustacia is talking with a man, he listens for a while from under the bank. Then he decides to brave the strange light and noise after all, rather than incur Miss Eustacia's wrath at being interrupted. As he marches stoutly back along the path, he finds that the light and the noise are gone.

As he comes upon the sandpit, he sees a lighted van. He ascends a slope of the pit so he can peer into the open door of the wagon. "By a stove inside the van sat a figure red from head to heels.... He was darning a stocking, which was red like the rest of him ... as he darned he smoked a pipe, the stem and bowl of which were red also." Hearing movements of the ponies outside, the reddleman comes to the door just as Johnny, stepping on ground that gives way, rolls down the bank to his very feet. By questioning Johnny, the reddleman learns matters of importance to him: that Johnny was given a sixpence by Miss Vye to keep up her bonfire; that a gentleman came to talk with her; that she "told him that she supposed he had not married the other woman because he liked his old sweetheart best"; and that the gentleman had "said he did like her best" and was coming to see her again under Rainbarrow. Johnny now pleads to be allowed to go home. The reddleman, having learned what he wants to know, leads Johnny onto the path, and then returns inside to his darning.

Comment

Hardy's use of dialogue between little Johnny Nunsuch and Diggory Venn serves to tighten the plot. Diggory gets the information he needs about Wildeve and Eustacia to help him from his plans to protect Thomasin. We are now set to have the forces of the mind plot against the forces of the heart.

CHAPTER 9: LOVE LEADS A SHREWD MAN INTO STRATEGY

We learn that Diggory Venn, reddleman, is in love with Thomasin Yeobright. He reads over a letter from Thomasin written two years ago. Diggory, at that time a dairy farmer, had asked her to marry him. Her letter, a gentle refusal, had caused him to give up dairy farming and adopt the reddle trade. But in his wanderings he manages to be often in Thomasin's heath-near her, yet never intruding. He is happy that he is the one she trusted to help her on this day. He is doubtful of Wildeve's intentions, but Thomasin wants him, and Diggory Venn is "determined to aid her to be happy in her own chosen way."

He decides to spy upon Eustacia Vye, whom he regards as a conspirator against Thomasin's happiness. For the next six nights he goes to stand "behind a hollybush on the edge of the pit not twenty yards from Rainbarrow ... but he watched in vain." The seventh night he sees "a female shape floating along the ridge and the outline of a young man ascending from the valley." Covering himself with a blanket of turves, he creeps along on his stomach till he is very close to where Eustacia and Damon Wildeve have met. Wildeve is asking Eustacia if he should marry Thomasin. He wishes "Tamsie were not such a confoundedly good little woman so that I could be faithful to you without injuring a worthy person." Eustacia asks him why he has not married Thomasin: "Perhaps it was not for love of me you did not marry her." He replies that "the immediate reason was that the license would not do for the place, and before I could get another she ran away.... Since then her aunt has spoken to me in a tone which I don't like at all."

Eustacia is enraged that he will not admit a consuming passion for her. He accuses her of treating him cruelly when he did love her, while she maintains he loves her still. "You will love me all your life long. You would jump to marry me!" He now confesses he would. Wildeve presses her to leave the heath, which they both abhor, and go to America with him. She begs for time to think about it, and they walk away out of hearing. Diggory Venn, troubled, throws off his blanket of turves and walks back to his van. "My Tamsie" (he speaks to himself), "what can be done? Yes, I will see that Eustacia Vye."

Comment

Now we know why Diggory Venn is so much interested in the affair of Wildeve and Eustacia. His love for Thomasin transforms him from a humble, unassuming reddleman into a man of action. He unashamedly eavesdrops, and hears Eustacia reveal indecision to be her weakness. Wildeve is ready to marry her and take her to America, but "America is so far away." She has the chance to escape the hated heath. Does she take it? No. Though she passionately loves Wildeve, her pride will not let her marry a man she considers inferior.

CHAPTER 10: A DESPERATE ATTEMPT AT PERSUASION

Early the next morning Diggory Venn emerges from his van and sets out for Mistover Knap. He is determined to have an interview with Miss Vye. As he enters the garden, he encounters Captain Vye gazing through his telescope at the English Channel.

They greet each other, and Venn explains that his business is with Miss Vye, but the captain rebukes him for calling so early on a lady. The reddleman says he will wait around, hoping that she will see him. After a long time, Eustacia comes out and walks leisurely toward him. She allows him to walk beside her and explain his mission.

Venn brings all his strategy into play. First, he tells her his fear that, because of another woman, Wildeve may not marry Thomasin. He appeals to her power over men to persuade Wildeve to give up the other woman and marry Thomasin. When Eustacia denies her influence and claims disinterest in the marriage, he appeals to her vanity. He insists that her comeliness must enable her to twist Wildeve to her will, but Eustacia says: "Surely what she cannot do who has been so much with him I cannot do living up here away from him." Diggory's next move is to confront her with the truth: "The woman that stands between Wildeve and Thomasin is yourself." He urges her to give up Wildeve as beneath her. She replies impetuously, "I will not be beaten down by an inferior woman ... he was mine before he was hers. He came back-because-because he liked me best!"

Diggory Venn now tries a new tack. He appeals to her hatred of the heath. "Now Budmouth is a wonderful place-out of every ten folks you meet nine of 'em in love. Now I could get you there." He explains that he knows of a rich widow-lady who wants a companion, but Eustacia refuses to consider working. She says, "O if I could live in a gay town as a lady should and go my own way and do my own things, I'd give the wrinkled half of my life." Diggory begs her to help him "get Thomasin happy and the chance shall be yours." She scorns the thought and dismisses him. Then she wanders alone to the bank and, gazing down over the vale in the direction of Wildeve's inn, speaks passionately: "I will never give him up-never!"

Comment

Here we enjoy the fencing between the imperious Eustacia and the now purposeful Diggory Venn. Eustacia again shows her weakness to be indecision. She can escape the heath by going to the popular seaside resort she remembers so ecstatically, but only if she will go as a companion. Surely this will fire her imagination and ensure her escape. But no. Her pride will not let her lower herself to work. She is too proud to compromise. She is also caught in a web of her own weaving. "The man (Wildeve) who had begun by being merely her amusement, and would never have been more than her hobby but for his skill in deserting her at the right moments, was now again her desire." Eustacia and Wildeve are playing cat and mouse.

CHAPTER 11: THE DISHONEST OF AN HONEST WOMAN

As Diggory Venn walks despondently back to his van, he meets Mrs. Yeobright walking slowly toward the Quiet Woman Inn. He discovers that Mrs. Yeobright is going to Wildeve for the same purpose as his own in going to see Eustacia. He asks her to give up her plan and instead to consider himself as the man to marry her niece. He confesses his love and tells her of his past proposal. Mrs. Yeobright is surprised, but she still feels Thomasin should marry the man she loves. As she goes on toward the Inn "she thanked God for the weapon which the reddleman had put into her hands." Calling upon Wildeve, she reveals to him that another man wishes to marry Thomasin - and that she would not like to encourage the other man unless Wildeve will promise not to interfere. Wildeve reflects uncomfortably upon this new turn of events, then asks for time to think it over. Mrs. Yeobright agrees to give him a day or two, provided he will not communicate with Thomasin.

Mrs. Yeobright's visit sends Wildeve to Eustacia that very night. He presses her to marry him, then admits that Mrs. Yeobright has asked him to give up Thomasin. Now it is Eustacia's turn to play hard-to-get. Languidly, she asks for time to decide. He says, "You loved me a month ago warmly enough to go anywhere with me." She counters with "And you loved Thomasin." He replies, "Yes, perhaps that was where the reason lay. I don't hate her now." To which Eustacia responds, "Exactly. The only thing is that you no longer can get her." He pleads with her, but she still asks for time. Granting her a week to make up her mind, Wildeve leaves. As Eustacia walks back into the house, she is greeted by her grandfather with the news that young Clym Yeobright "is coming home next week to spend Christmas with his mother." Eustacia asks where he has been living. Her grandfather replies, "In that rookery of pomp and vanity, Paris."

Comment

Now we have Mrs. Yeobright joining in the conspiracy. Shrewdly, she holds Venn's proposal to Thomasin as a threat over Wildeve - and Wildeve, like Eustacia, discovers desire for the hard-to-get. He is exasperated by the aunt's demands, but now that Thomasin is wanted by another, he wants her himself. Nonetheless, he makes one more try for Eustacia. Eustacia, however, finding out that Thomasin may escape Wildeve, now loses her own ardor. "You come to get me because you cannot get her." We begin to feel that, for Eustacia, it is always to be "the road not taken." She will not go to Budmouth, because to become a companion would be beneath her. She will not go to America, because it is too far away. She loses her ardor for Wildeve when she thinks him discarded by another. She cannot make compromises.

Summary: Hardy, the architect, has a masterly way of building his characters almost stone by stone:

1.   In the first chapter we meet the heath - and the heath alone.

2.   In the second chapter we meet two "unknown" persons (and a concealed third). The heath is sketched again, this time through the eyes of one of the "unknowns," the reddleman. We see the shadow of the heroine.

3.   The third chapter introduces us to the common folk of the heath. We take part in their heath revels; we hear their gossip about the "gentry." Thus indirectly we get to know about the major characters without yet encountering them as such. The reddleman appears again briefly, and we get a glimpse of Mrs. Yeobright.

4.   The fourth chapter gives us Mrs. Yeobright. As she meets Diggory Venn and finds her niece, Thomasin, in his van, the plot of the story begins to unravel.

5.   Chapter Five adds to our understanding of Mrs. Yeobright and Thomasin, and introduces Wildeve. Wildeve, we decide, is going to be a character ruled by emotions. In this chapter we have an accumulation of most of the heath people we have met so far - a sort of summing up.

6.   Chapter Six introduces Eustacia Vye, the sultry heroine. The plot intrigue is revealed as we listen in on Eustacia's meeting with Wildeve.

7.   In Chapter Seven, Hardy builds for us a powerful word picture of Eustacia Vye.

8. Chapter Eight helps the story by getting Diggory Venn into the plot. He must save his heroine from the villain. (His heroine is Thomasin; his villain is Eustacia.)

9. Chapter Nine reveals Venn's love for Thomasin.

10. The remaining chapters show us the strategy: Mrs. Yeobright fences with Wildeve; Diggory Venn fences with Eustacia Vye; Eustacia Vye and Damon Wildeve fence with each other. The ingenuous Thomasin stays unobtrusively in the background. Book One has developed all the characters of the heath to the point where we are ready for the grand entrance of the hero: Clym Yeobright, the Native who Returns-from Paris.

THE RETURN OF THE NATIVE

BOOK SECOND: THE ARRIVAL

· ·

CHAPTER 1: TIDINGS OF THE COMER

One fine November afternoon, Eustacia Vye overhears two heath men talking with her grandfather. The men are busy stacking furze-faggots for the Vyes' winter fuel; the old captain is looking on. Eustacia, inside the house, hears the voices coming down the chimney, which is near the furze-stack. They are talking of Clym Yeobright "The young man has settled in Paris. Manager to a diamond merchant, or some such thing, is he not?" They speak of Clym's book learning, and add, "Now I should think cap'n, that Miss Eustacia had about as much in her head that comes from books as anybody about here?" Captain Vye gruffly remarks that Miss Eustacia would be better off is she "had less romantic nonsense in her head." With that, he walks away. The two men agree between themselves that "she and Clym Yeobright would make a very pretty pigeon pair-hey?... Clym's family is as good as hers.... Nothing would please me better than to see them two man and wife." We learn that Clym is coming to Budmouth by steamer. The two men then speak of the "bad trouble about his cousin Thomasin." One says, "I've heard she wouldn't have Wildeve now if he asked her." The men move away, leaving Eustacia entranced. "A young and clever man was coming into the lonely heath from... Paris.... the heath men had instinctively coupled her and this man together in their minds as a pair born for each other. That five minutes of overhearing furnished Eustacia with visions enough to fill the whole blank afternoon." At dusk she decides to take her usual walk, this time in the direction of Clym's mother's house at Blooms-End.

Comment

One significant fact learned in this chapter is that Eustacia is nineteen years old. We realize that, with her particular nature, what she has overheard will affect her strongly. To have it mentioned that Thomasin won't have Wildeve will definitely lessen her desire for him. Of course, the men's conviction that she and Clym would make a perfect pair, well-matched in family and education, starts her day-dreaming and plotting for a meeting with this "man coming from heaven." An added interest for us is how his mother's simple cottage will seem to this man returning from the center of the fashionable world.

CHAPTER 2: THE PEOPLE AT BLOOMS-END MAKE READY

Meanwhile, at Blooms-End cottage, Thomasin and her aunt are preparing the house for Clym. Up in the barn loft together collecting apples for the holiday, they talk. Mrs. Yeobright bemoans the fact that Thomasin did not return Clym's love. Thomasin is spirited about the villagers' attitude toward her incomplete wedding. "Why don't people judge me by my acts?

Now, look at me as I kneel here, picking up these apples - do I look like a lost woman? ... I wish all good women were as good as I!" Mrs. Yeobright answers justly: "Strangers don't see you as I do, they judge from false reports. Well, it is a silly job, and I am partly to blame."

As soon as the apples are collected, they set forth over the heath to gather holly, Mrs. Yeobright asks Thomasin if she will walk with her to meet Clym this evening. Thomasin replies that she wants to - "Elsie it would seem as if I had forgotten him." But she adds: "I belong to one man; nothing can alter that. And that man I must marry for my pride's sake." She goes on talking defensively about Wildeve. Mrs. Yeobright tries to get her to admit that her love has changed toward him. All Thomasin will say is "He wished to marry me, and I wish to marry him." Mrs. Yeobright tells her: "Well, wait till he repeats his offer," adding that she believes he will, because she has told him "he is standing in the way of another lover of yours." Thomasin is astonished. She commands her aunt to say nothing to Clym about all this until after Christmas. The two women walk home "each bearing half the gathered boughs."

Comment

Here Thomasin shows herself to be a far stronger person than we have believed her to be. She expresses herself with conviction and commands her aunt with authority. We find that she has had three men in love with her. Actually, at this point, Eustacia and Thomasin vie in our minds for first place as heroine of the novel. The quiet, unassuming Thomasin decides what she wants and is ready to make sacrifices to get it: her pride must be restored by her marriage to Wildeve. The showy, impulsive Eustacia flashes here, flashes there, never allowing herself to come to grips with life-backing down whenever forced to make a decision. What different creatures they are!

CHAPTER 3: HOW A LITTLE SOUND PRODUCED A GREAT DREAM

Eustacia is standing just at the edge of the heath near Mrs. Yeobright's cottage. She has decided that the guest has not yet come, and is about to turn back, when she hears sounds of people approaching. It is now too dark for her to see who is coming, but, as they pass, she recognizes the voices of Mrs. Yeobright and Thomasin. The third voice comes to her in a greeting, directed to her shadowy form standing aside, just off the path. A masculine voice calls out to her, "Good night!" As the voices pass on, she hears their words but attends only to one: "the voice that … wished her good night…. Once it surprised her notions by remarking upon the friendliness and geniality written in the faces of the hills around."

Eustacia is astounded long after the voices have faded into the distance. "What could the tastes of that man be who saw friendliness and geniality in these shaggy hills?" Upon returning home, she asks her grandfather why they have never been friendly with the Yeobrights. He replies that her "town tastes would find them far too countrified." He believes that he once accidentally offended Mrs. Yeobright, and he has not seen her since. Eustacia determines to meet Clym. Hoping to come upon him, she takes "an airing two or three times a day upon the Egdon hills." On five different days she sallies forth, only to be disappointed. She begins to feel ashamed of her weakness in pursuing him and resolves to look for him no more. But Providence is coquettish.

Comment

We realize that Eustacia will scheme and maneuver until she has woven Clym Yeobright into her web. She is infused with zeal for the purpose by her belief that he fulfills two necessary requirements: he is worthy of her, and he will take her to the exotic life of Paris.

CHAPTER 4: EUSTACIA IS LED ON TO AN ADVENTURE

Eustacia is haunted by the "awakening voice" - the voice that has said two words to her - "good night." She tries to think how to meet the owner of the voice. As she is sitting alone musing in the dusk by the fire, someone knocks at the door. It is a heath boy, Charley, "one of the Egdon mummers for this year." (A mummer is a masked person taking part in a folk-play.) Charley asks if the mummers may practice in Captain Vye's fuel house, as they have done before. Permission given, the mummers assemble at seven o'clock to practice the play, "Saint George and the Turkish Knight." Eustacia goes to the shed lean-to to watch the rehearsal through a knot-hole in the wall, and learns that the first performance will be at Mrs. Yeobright's party for Clym on Monday night.

The mummers prepare to leave. Eustacia returns to the fireside just before Charley comes to give back the key. Eustacia, inviting Charley to sit with her, asks him to say his lines of the Turkish Knight. Then, when he finishes, she repeats the lines exactly and with great fervor. Charley is astonished. "Well, you be a clever lady! I've been three weeks learning mine." She admits to having heard them before - and then asks Charley if he will let her play his part on Monday night. "What should I have to give you to lend me your things, to let me take your place for an hour or two ... and on no account to say a word about who or what I am? She offers money, but the lad shakes his head. He asks for half an hour of "holding your hand in mine." She bargains for a quarter of an hour.

He agrees, saying, "if I may kiss it too."

The next evening Charley appears, bringing the trappings of the Turkish Knight and asking for his payment. Eustacia leans against the doorpost of the fuel house and gives him her gloved hand. "Charley took it in both his own with a tenderness ... like that of a child holding a captured sparrow. "Why there's a glove on it! '" She agrees "it is hardly fair," and pulls the glove off. They stand without speaking for six or eight minutes, until Charley says, "I think I won't use it all up tonight. May I have the other few minutes at another time?" Eustacia replies, "As you like, but it must be over in a week." She sends Charley to walk in the garden, while she changes to the Turkish Knight. Then she calls him back to hear her rehearse her lines. They plan that she shall take his place at the last minute before the next rehearsal. He asks for "one minute more of what I am owed." Eustacia gives him her hand and, starting to count, reaches seven or eight minutes. "There, 'tis all gone; and I didn't mean quite all," sighs Charley. "Well, 'tis over, and now I'll get home-along."

Comment

"A traditional pastime is to be distinguished from a mere revival ... in this, that while in the revival all is excitement and fervor, the survival is carried on with a stolidity and an absence of stir." Thus Hardy describes what might be a formal presentation of a Mummers' Play as contrasted with the oft-repeated custom shown in these chapters.

In the United States we often have what Hardy calls "a mere revival" of the Mummers' Play. This is a formal presentation given at Christmas time. The mummers troop through the audience up to the stage carrying decorations and food, as they sing appropriate songs, such as: "Deck the Halls with Boughs of Holly," "The Boar's Head in Hand Bring I," and "The Twelve Days of Christmas." After the stage is set, piece by piece, the action of the play begins with each character announcing himself in verse. The play follows the same pattern as the "traditional pastime" version described in the comment to Chapter Five, but the audience is a formal one, whereas in Mrs. Yeobright's home we have an informal atmosphere and no artificiality of stage and hall.

CHAPTER 5: THROUGH THE MOONLIGHT

When the mummers have assembled at the fuel house the next evening and are wondering where Charley is, Eustacia makes her entrance. "Here's Charley at last! How late you be, Charley." "'Tis not Charley," says the Turkish Knight, "'Tis a cousin of Miss Vye's, come to take Charley's place out of curiosity. He was obliged to go and look for the heath-croppers." The play is hastily rehearsed, and the mummers are "delighted with the new knight." They set out for Mrs. Yeobright's cottage. Arriving, they hear lively dancing going on inside. They wait outside till the dance is over, then Father Christmas leads them in. After greetings, the play begins. When it is the Turkish Knight's turn to be slain, Eustacia manages to fall in a relatively upright position against the clock case, so she can look around for Clym.

Comment

Mummers are masked players who go from house to house at festival times to give amusement. In England the Mummers' Plays may have come from the traditional sword dances. Begun in the eighteenth century, Mummers' Plays are customarily given at Christmastime. The characters are always men, and include: St. George, the hero; the Turkish Knight; Captain Slasher; the Valiant Soldier; the Saracen; and the Doctor. Sometimes the Turkish Knight is replaced by a Dragon: Then the play is known as *St. George and the Dragon*. The group is led in by Father Christmas, who gives a genial introduction in **rhyme**. Each character introduces himself in rhyme: "In come I...." Then comes the dueling. The Turkish Knight slays Captain Slasher; St. George slays the Turkish Knight and then slays the Saracen. After the dueling, the Doctor revives the slain warriors. Father Christmas gives a rhyming finish to the play. A collection is taken and refreshments are served to the mummers before they leave.

Hardy uses the Mummers' Play in this instance as a colorful way of bringing about the meeting of his hero and heroine, Clym and Eustacia. It also adds authenticity to the feeling of the heath countryside and the heath people.

CHAPTER 6: THE TWO STAND FACE TO FACE

As Eustacia looks around, she finds that Thomasin is not present. She remembers that a light was shining from an upstairs room. Grandfer Cantle is sitting inside the settle, in the warmest spot, but Eustacia is interested in the tall figure of Clym Yeobright "leaning against the settle's outer end." She is pleased with what she sees. As the play ends and the mummers sit down to eat, Clym comes to offer food to the Turkish Knight. In order not to have to unmask she refuses, but she does accept wine, which she can drink under her disguise. As she sips, she watches Clym go into another room where she can see a door open and Thomasin appear briefly. Eustacia hears how kindly and earnestly Clym speaks with Thomasin. When he disappears into another room with her, Eustacia regrets her disguise and her inability to charm Clym away from Thomasin.

Frustrated, she feels she must escape. She slips outside to wait for the mummers at the gate, and in a few minutes Clym Yeobright comes out. He bluntly asks her if she is a woman. She admits it. He asks why she has done this. She answers that life has depressed her, and she wants excitement. He questions her further, but she will not reveal her identity. He leaves, and Eustacia, waiting no longer for the mummers, wanders along home. As she proceeds, she members that this is the night she was to have met Wildeve on Rainbarrow to give her answer to his pleading for elopement. He has waited in vain. "Well, so much the better: it did not hurt him." She recalls Thomasin's winning manner toward her cousin Clym, and speaks aloud: "O that she (Thomasin) had been married to Damon before this! And she would have been if it hadn't been for me! If I had only known - if I had only known!"

We can see how Eustacia, passionate by nature, and wearied of her former lover, is ripe and eager for adventure with a new man; especially one who seems by hearsay to fulfill all her romantic hopes for a mate. Events in this chapter serve to strengthen her resolve to get Clym Yeobright for herself. We feel his fate is sealed.

CHAPTER 7: A COALITION BETWEEN BEAUTY AND ODDNESS

When, the next day, her grandfather inquires why she was out so late the night before, Eustacia tells him, "I wanted an adventure, and I went with the mummers. I played the part of the Turkish Knight." Her grandfather is delighted: "Eustacia, you never did - ha! ha! Dammy, how 'twould have pleased me forty years ago! But remember no more of it, my girl … no figuring in breeches again." Eustacia agrees.

Her next walk takes her to the neighborhood of the reddleman's van. Meeting him on the heath, she boldly asks him about his approaching marriage to Miss Yeobright. She finds out what she wants to know - that the reddleman does not know of the marriage, and is being used by Mrs. Yeobright to rekindle the fire of Wildeve's desire for Thomasin. She is about to walk on when she sees Wildeve approaching, though he is not located where he can see her. She asks Venn if she may rest in his van for a few minutes. While she is thus concealed, Wildeve passes by. The reddleman informs Eustacia and, realizing she had plotted to sidestep Wildeve, tells her how he observed Wildeve last night waiting on Rainbarrow "for a lady who didn't come." Eustacia assures Diggory that Wildeve will be disappointed again tonight. She enlists Venn to carry to Wildeve a note and a "few little things" which she wishes returned to him. Returning to her home, she brings back a parcel and a note.

These the reddleman takes to Wildeve waiting on Rainbarrow. After Wildeve has read the letter, he remarks, "I am made a great fool of, one way and another. Do you know what is in this letter?" The reddleman merely hums a tune: "Ru-um-tum-tum." Wildeve, looking carefully at Venn, says, "Well, I suppose I deserve it, considering how I have played with them both." He asks why Venn should be sending him courting Thomasin again when "Mrs. Yeobright says you are to marry her." Diggory, astonished replies "Good Lord! I heard of this before, but didn't believe it. When did she say so?" Now it is Wildeve's turn to hum a tune: "Ru-um-tum-tum." "O Lord - how we can imitate!" Venn says contemptuously. "I'll have this out. I'll go straight to her." He hurries back to the van to change his clothes, but Wildeve is too quick for him.

By the time Diggory Venn gets to Mrs. Yeobright's cottage, Wildeve is just coming from it. "You may as well go back again now. I've claimed her and got her. Good night, reddleman!"

Comment

We see how ruthless and unscrupulous Eustacia can be when she is determined to have her way. She feels no qualms about throwing over Wildeve. She is happy to maneuver him into rushing to marry Thomasin, thus getting her safely out of Clym's way. In all justice to her, however, we must remember that Wildeve had tossed her aside to marry Thomasin in the first place.

CHAPTER 8: FIRMNESS IS DISCOVERED IN A GENTLE HEART

Thomasin has met Wildeve just outside the cottage and agreed to marry him. Going inside, she tells her aunt the news. "He would like the wedding to be the day after tomorrow, quite privately; at the church of his parish - not at ours." Thomasin says she has agreed. "I am a practical woman now. I don't believe in hearts at all. I would marry him under any circumstances since - since Clym's letter." (Clym Yeobright, away for a ten days' visit, having heard the gossip about Thomasin and Wildeve, has written that he cannot understand or believe it: "It is too ridiculous that such a girl as Thomasin could so mortify us as to get jilted on the wedding day.") Mrs. Yeobright and Thomasin are discussing the details of the wedding when Diggory Venn's knock is heard. Mrs. Yeobright goes out to talk with him. Coming back inside, she tells Thomasin: "Another lover has come to ask for you.... I told him be was too late." Thomasin breathes a sigh, "Poor Diggory."

The morning arrives for the wedding. Thomasin braids her hair in a seven-strand braid, dons her blue silk dress, and at nine o'clock is ready to leave. She prefers to go alone. Mrs. Yeobright blesses her and sends an old slipper flying after her. Half an hour later Clym comes home from the opposite direction, and he and Mrs. Yeobright talk about Thomasin over breakfast. Clym cannot understand why he was not told of the first wedding preparations. He feels his mother was wrong in not telling him. He decides he must go to see that all is well with Thomasin.

He soon comes back, however, accompanied by Diggory Venn. Venn has been to the wedding and is coming to tell them about it. We learn that Miss Vye gave Thomasin away. Diggory had seen her walking among the headstones outside the church. He went inside and, sitting out of sight in the gallery, saw Eustacia enter. "The parson looked round before beginning, and as she was the only near he beckoned to her, and she went up to the rails." Having told his version, the reddleman left the house, and thereafter was seen on Egdon Heath no more for months. But one event of the wedding has escaped him. "When Thomasin was ... engaged in signing her name, Wildeve had flung towards Eustacia a glance that said plainly, 'I have punished you now.' She had replied in a low tone ... 'You mistake; it gives me sincerest pleasure to see her your wife today'."

Comment

Thomasin reveals in this chapter that she is no longer an ingenuous, romantic maiden. I do not plead for him, aunt," she remarks of Wildeve, "human nature is weak, and I am not a blind woman to insist that he is perfect. I did think so, but I don't know.... I hope for the best." In about two months' time, Thomasin has become a woman resigned to disappointment. A very interesting custom of the country folk is explained in this chapter: the braiding of a woman's hair according to a calendar system - "the more important the day the more numerous the strands in the braid." On ordinary working days there were

three strands; on Sundays four; at special festivals, such as May-
polings, five. Thomasin "had said that when she married, she
would braid" her hair in seven strands.

This chapter gives a backward glance at what might have
been, and a forewarning of what is to come, when Clym says: "Do
you know, mother ... I once thought of Tamsin as a sweetheart?
Yes, I did.... And when I came home and saw her this time she
seemed so much more affectionate than usual, that I was quite
reminded of those days, particularly on the night of the party,
when she was unwell. We had the party just the same - was
not that rather cruel to her?" To Mrs. Yeobright's reply that she
had felt it wise not to make more gloom by postponing it, Clym
answers: "I almost wish you had not had that party, and for other
reasons." We believe he is thinking of the "unknown woman" at
the party; and we see how women's schemes can change the
course of men's lives.

Summary: Hardy builds his plot almost architecturally;
in this book it develops thought by thought in the mind of
Eustacia Vye:

1. Eustacia hears of Clym Yeobright through the heath
men's gossip. She decides he is worthy of her.

2. Thomasin reveals her determination to marry Wildeve.
She unknowingly aids Eustacia's plan by requesting secrecy.
Clym must not know of Wildeve's connection with her.

3. Eustacia's passionate nature is aroused by hearing
Clym's voice. We realize that Clym loves the heath. Knowing
Eustacia's hatred of the heath, we wonder if she will get what
she wants from Clym. We feel sure she is going to get him - but
will she get Paris, also?

4.   Eustacia schemes to get a look at Clym (who is still only a voice to her). She arranges to go to Mrs. Yeobright's party with the mummers, disguised as the Turkish Knight.

5.   The actual production of the Mummers' Play, *St. George and the Turkish Knight*, parallels the Guy Fawkes Day celebration as a custom of the country.

6.   Eustacia, at the party, has her opportunity to see Clym. Now it is his turn to be lured by a voice - the voice of the Turkish Knight, who refuses his offer of refreshments and who, he decides, is a woman. He follows her outside to learn her identity. She strengthens her cause by refusing to reveal herself, leaving him with his curiosity aroused, convinced that she is a cultured and fascinating woman.

7.   Eustacia now plots skillfully to get rid of Wildeve and Thomasin, so that her way is clear to get Clym.

8.   Thomasin marries Wildeve; Eustacia, with great satisfaction, gives her away.

THE RETURN OF THE NATIVE

BOOK THIRD: THE FASCINATION

CHAPTER 1: MY MIND TO ME A KINGDOM IS

Here we have a detailed description of Clym. As a lad he was original in his thoughts. At six "he had asked a Scripture riddle: 'Who was the first man known to wear breeches?' ... At seven he painted the Battle of Waterloo with tiger-lily pollen and black currant juice." By the time he was twelve he had achieved a reputation as a scholar and an artist. When his father died a neighboring gentleman had taken an interest in him, sending him to Budmouth, London, and Paris.

Now he is at home on vacation. The villagers are wondering why he remains so long among them. On a Sunday morning walk he comes upon the regular weekly outdoor haircutting. Fairway, the barber, admits the men have been talking about Clym, wondering why he stays at home so long. Clym tells them his heath home-coming has made him discover that his Paris business is "the idlest, vainest, most effeminate business that ever a man could be put to." He has decided to give it up for "some rational occupation.... I shall keep a school as near to Egdon as possible ... and have a night-school in my mother's house. But I must study a little at first, to get properly qualified." As he walks on, the neighbors express disbelief. One remarks, "'Tis good-hearted of the young man, but, for my part, I think he had better mind his business."

Comment

Another interesting custom of the country is described in detail in this chapter: the Sunday morning hair-cutting. The local barbering was always done at the same hour on this day outdoors in front of Timothy Fairway's house. The victim sat "on a chopping block in front of the house, without a coat ... the neighbors gossiping around, idly observing the locks of hair as they rose upon the wind ... and flew away." The Sunday hair-cutting was followed by "the great Sunday wash ... at noon, which in its turn was followed by the great Sunday dressing an hour later. On Egdon Heath Sunday proper did not begin till dinner time, and even then it was a somewhat battered specimen of the day." We can tell that the men gathered at the barbering are not impressed by Clym's decision to remain among them to teach. We wonder how successful his mission will be.

CHAPTER 2: THE NEW COURSE CAUSES DISAPPOINTMENT

Clym is further described. He is a product of the heath and loves it well. "His toys had been the flint-knives and arrowheads which he found there ... his flowers, the purple bells and yellow gorse; his animal kingdom, the snakes and croppers [heath ponies]....

Take all the varying hates felt by Eustacia Vye towards the heath, and translate them into loves, and you have the heart of Clym." Upon reaching home on Sunday, Clym tells his mother of his decision to stay and teach. She is disturbed that he wants to "go backward in the world." He insists that, as a schoolmaster, he can do something worthy before he dies. Christian Cantle comes in to tell them that Susan Nunsuch stuck a long stocking-needle into Miss Vye at church, because Miss Vye was bewitching Susan's children. Clym says to his mother, "Do you think I have turned teacher too soon?" Later in the day, Sam, the turf-cutter, stops by to borrow a long rope. "The captain's bucket has dropped into the well, and they are in want of water." Clym goes out with him, asking about Miss Vye. Sam describes her as a handsome girl. "Do you think she would like to teach children?" asks Clym. Sam thinks not, but tells Clym how he might judge for himself: "We are going to grapple for the bucket at six o'clock, and you could lend a hand.... She's sure to be walking around." Clym says he will think about it.

Comment

Now it is Clym's turn to scheme to see Eustacia Vye. This chapter parallels Book Second, Chapter 4, where Eustacia schemed, with Charley, to see Clym at the party. We realize what contrasting natures and urges these two people have: Eustacia hates the heath, Clym loves it; Eustacia wants the glitter of Paris, Clym wishes to turn his back on all that.

CHAPTER 3: THE FIRST ACT IN A TIMEWORN DRAMA

Clym and his mother walk over the heath together. She is going to see Thomasin; he decides to go on to Mistover to help raise the well-bucket. Mrs. Yeobright watches him go with misgivings: "There is no help for it…. They are sure to see each other." Clym finds Timothy Fairway directing the proceedings at the captain's well. The bucket keeps slipping away into the well. Yeobright offers to spell Fairway for a time. As Clym kneels and leans over the well, a soft voice is heard: "Tie a rope round him - it is dangerous!" Clym recognizes the voice as "that of the melancholy mummer." "How thoughtful of her," he thinks to himself. Finally the well bucket is retrieved.

One of the men goes to tell the captain, but finds only Eustacia at home. She comes out to ask: "Will it be possible to draw water here tonight?" It seems not, because the bottom of the bucket is knocked out. The men leave, but Clym stays on to arrange about getting her some water. She refuses to drink the pool water: "I am managing to exist in a wilderness, but I cannot drink from a pond." Between them, Clym and Eustacia manage to lower a pail, but Eustacia's hand is burned by the rope. This is the second time she has been wounded today. Clym speaks of the **episode** at church, saying, "I blush for my native Egdon. Was it a serious injury you received in church, Miss Vye?" He speaks so sympathetically that Eustacia rolls up her sleeve to show him the wound. She says she shall not go to church again: "I cannot face their eyes after this." Clym tells her that he has "come to clean away these cobwebs. Would you like to help me - by high class teaching?" She is not so inclined, feeling hatred for them all. He thinks if she were to hear his scheme she might relent. It seems time for them to part. Clym makes bold to mention that they have met before. Eustacia says, "I do not own it." He speaks of the heath as "exhilarating, and strengthening, and soothing." She calls it a "cruel taskmaster." He tells of a curious druidical (ancient Celtic priest) stone out on the heath; she asks about the boulevards in Paris. They separate.

Clym returns home to unpack his books and lamps. He is up early and ready to study to next morning. By sunset he goes for a walk on the heath. Returning after dusk, he admits to his mother that he has been to meet Eustacia Vye. His mother wishes he had walked another way so he would not get mixed up with one she calls a hussy; but, she says, "I have been thinking that you might get on as a schoolmaster and rise that way...." A few days later a barrow (ancient mound covering graves) is opened on the heath. Christian Cantle, Mrs. Yeobright's gardener, passes by the site on his way to his work. He tells Mrs. Yeobright that they found some pots of "real skellington bones," that Mr. Yeobright was going to bring one home, but on second thought he gave it away to Miss Vye. When Clym returns, Mrs. Yeobright confronts him with "The urn you had meant for me you gave away." Clym does not reply. He continues to study and take long walks, after which he and his mother eat in silence. Finally, during the month of March, he confesses he has seen Eustacia many times. He believes that with an educated wife like her, he can "establish a good private school for farmers' sons." His mother calls him blinded by this "hussy." Clym flushes and, rising to leave the house, tells his mother, "I won't hear it. I may be led to answer you in a way which we shall both regret."

Comment

Two interesting procedures are explained in this chapter. One is the method of raising a well bucket. Timothy Fairway, secured by a rope around his waist, takes the lead, and half a dozen men help in the hauling. Fairway leans far down the well to swing the rope to which the grapnel (an anchor-like hook) is attached. Round and round it is swung till it finally catches onto something. Then all hands haul on the line to bring up the object. The first time, the well bucket is caught, but only by the edge of the hoop, so that it slips away again. The next time, the grapnel hooks onto a coil of rope instead of the bucket. At the third try, the bucket is successfully hooked and successfully hauled to the top. Procedure number two is the opening of a barrow. Barrows are man-made mounds which cover graves. Christian Cantle describes the opening: "They have dug a hole, and they have found things like flower pots upside down ... and inside these be real charnel bones. They have carried 'em off to men's houses; but I shouldn't like to sleep where they will bide. Dead folks have been known to come out and claim their own." In addition to these detailed descriptions of heath country events, this chapter shows a mother fighting for her son. First Mrs. Yeobright tries to dissuade Clyms from attaching himself to any woman at present - then she boldly denounces Eustacia as unworthy of him. Clym is tactless in revealing to his mother the new woman in his life; Mrs. Yeobright is unwise in expressing so heatedly her opinion of Eustacia.

CHAPTER 4: AN HOUR OF BLISS AND MANY HOURS OF SADNESS

Clym and his mother are no longer speaking, except on passing matters. He, trying to keep up a show of conversation, tells her of an eclipse of the moon. "I am going out to see it." Actually, we find that he and Eustacia have a tryst to meet on Rainbarrow, "ten minutes after the first mark of shade on the edge of the moon." Eustacia comes to the waiting Clym, to be enfolded in his arms. They speak of their love for each other. Eustacia is despondent; she fears Clym's mother will influence him against her. He reassures her and asks her to be his wife. She asks for time to think, and begs him to talk to her of Paris. He tells her of all the familiar places, and she begs him to go back to Paris again; if he will, she will promise to marry him. But he has vowed not to go back, and says, "Besides it would interfere with my scheme."

She says, "You will never adhere to your education plan, I am quite sure; and then it will be all right for me; and so I promise to be yours forever and ever." Clym is overjoyed. She warns him she will not make a "good homespun wife.... Don't mistake me, Clym: though I should like Paris, I love you for yourself alone. To be your wife and live in Paris would be heaven to me; but I would rather live with you in a hermitage here than not be yours at all." Hand in hand they return to Mistover. He regrets that it is too late to see her grandfather. They part reluctantly. As he walks home, Clym begins to see his problems: his mother's trust in him, his plan for becoming a teacher, and Eustacia's happiness. Just when his mother is beginning to accept his teaching scheme, he complicates her feelings by the addition of Eustacia.

Comment

Eustacia, whimsical creature though she is, is able to see more clearly than Clym how hazardous their life together will be. She must have him, but she knows he cannot hold her for long. She explicitly names his mother as the one that will estrange them, but she knows it will be her own passionate, will-o'-the-wisp nature that will defeat their love. Clym is an innocent when it comes to realizing the drives of a nature like Eustacia's. He believes he can pursue his studying and teaching, and also keep Eustacia happy, but Eustacia cannot bear to take second place to anyone or anything. Mrs. Yeobright is becoming reconciled to Clym's giving up the diamond business for teaching, but she can never become reconciled to Eustacia as the one to take her place in Clym's affections.

CHAPTER 5: SHARP WORDS ARE SPOKEN AND A CRISIS ENSUES

Now, Clym is either studying or meeting Eustacia in secret. Though Captain Vye knows of the engagement, no one else does. Mrs. Yeobright, however, comes home from visiting Thomasin one morning with the news. "The captain has let out at the woman that you and Eustacia are engaged to be married." Clym admits it. He means to keep a school in Budmouth when they are married. "My plan is one for instilling high knowledge into empty minds without first cramming them with what has to be uncrammed again before true study begins." His mother maintains stoutly that Eustacia is no wife to help him with this plan: "I hate the thought of any son of mine marrying badly! I wish I had never lived to see this; it is too much for me...." Clym is not able to endure her hard words. "I beg your pardon for having thought this my home. I will no longer inflict myself upon you; I'll go." Leaving the house, he walks to "a spot where a path emerged from one of the small hollows." Here he waits. Eustacia approaches, expecting to meet him and Mrs. Yeobright, for Clym had arranged with her to have such a meeting. He has to admit that his mother is irreconcilable to the idea of third marriage. Suddenly he decides: "We must be married at once; if you will agree to live in a tiny cottage somewhere on the heath until I take a house in Budmouth for the school, we can do it at a very little expense." Eustacia asks how long in a cottage. He replies, "about six months." So they agree to be married in two weeks.

Comment

Clym finds that he must cut off his relationship with his mother in order to have Eustacia. Mrs. Yeobright will not make any compromise. Feeling his known world crumbling, he must turn to his new love for strength. Eustacia is "no longer the goddess but the woman to him, a being to fight for, support, help, be maligned for." We catch a touch of foreboding in Hardy's closing words: "Whether Eustacia was to add one other to the list of those who love too hotly to love long and well, the forthcoming event was certainly a ready way of proving."

CHAPTER 6: YEOBRIGHT GOES AND THE BREACH IS COMPLETE

The next day, a wet, boisterous June day, having packed his things, Clym leaves his mother's home. He rents a small house near a village about five miles away and moves in. He is to be married on the twenty-fifth of June. Before he left home, he told his mother his plans and asked her to come and see them. She does not think it likely that she will. She is very much upset, and can do nothing but "walk up and down the garden path in a state bordering on stupefaction." Night gives her little rest. The next day she goes to her son's room to arrange it for his imaginary return. Thomasin comes to see her in the afternoon. Mrs. Yeobright inquires solicitously if Damon treats Thomasin well. Thomasin says he is "pretty fairly" kind to her, but "I want some money, you know, aunt-some to buy little things for myself - and he doesn't give me any." Her aunt tells her she must ask Wildeve to give her money. Mrs. Yeobright also tells Thomasin, however, that she has "a little box full of spade-guineas which your uncle put into my hands to divide between yourself and Clym." Thomasin asks for her share, but Mrs. Yeobright tells her to request money from Wildeve first "and see what he will do." Thomasin then tells her aunt she has heard about Clym's departure. The two women try to comfort each other, but Mrs. Yeobright inclines to self-pity and Thomasin calls her "too unyielding. Think how many mothers there are whose sons have brought them to public shame by real crimes." Mrs. Yeobright refuses to be comforted. All Thomasin can do is promise to come to see her each day. Wildeve learns of the coming wedding by seeing a van of goods passing the inn. The driver of the van tells him the things are going up to Captain Vye's, where there is "going to be a wedding." Wildeve is very much upset. "The old longing for Eustacia" reappears, chiefly because he now knows another man is to have her.

Comment

One of Hardy's especially fine descriptions is in this chapter. On the day Clym leaves home there is a June storm. "The young beeches were undergoing amputations, bruises, cripplings, and harsh lacerations, from which the wasting sap would bleed for many a day to come, and which would leave scars visible till the day of their burning. Each stem was wrenched at the root, where it moved like a bone in its socket, and at every onset of the gale convulsive sounds came from the branches as if pain were felt." So is the soul of Clym Yeobright tempest-tossed by the emotions aroused in him by the two women in his life. As a contrast to Clym, we see Wildeve as one "to be yearning for the difficult; to be weary of that offered; to care for the remote; to dislike the near."

CHAPTER 7: THE MORNING AND THE EVENING OF A DAY

We learn of the wedding through the feelings of Mrs. Yeobright. She is waiting at home for Thomasin to come for the money promised her. As she walks in the garden, she imagines the scene at the church; as her "old clock indoors whizzed forth twelve strokes," she hears faintly on the breeze the gay peal of the bells. "The ringers at East Egdon" are announcing the "nuptials of Eustacia and her son." (Bell ringers are men who, each holding one handbell, ring these bells singly in different patterns for various occasions.) Thomasin does not come, but toward evening Wildeve appears. Mrs. Yeobright treats him with "grim friendliness." He tells her that Thomasin was pressed to go to the wedding celebration at Mistover, so could not come as planned. "I believe you have something to give to Thomasin? If you like, I will take it." Mrs. Yeobright refuses to let him have it, saying it is "nothing worth troubling you with," Wildeve, quickly resentful, accuses her of doubting his honesty. When he leaves, Mrs. Yeobright considers what shall be the best way to get the money to Thomasin and to Clym.

Since they are both now at Mistover, she decides to send Christian Cantle with the two bags of money. She tells him exactly what is in the bags, so he will be impressed with their importance. As he journeys along toward Mistover, he hears voices on the heath, and takes the precaution of emptying the contents of the moneybags, one share into each boot. When he meets the voices, they turn out to be Fairway and several heath people he knows. They are going to "the raffle," at the Quiet Woman Inn, where "Every man puts in a shilling apiece, and one wins a gown-piece for his wife or sweetheart." Christian is persuaded to go along. He is also persuaded to "lay down his shilling," and he wins the gown-piece. He is so much impressed with his luck that he tells Wildeve about the money he is carrying, fancying his power over the dice "might do some good to a near relation of yours." Wildeve is alert at once. He offers to walk to Mistover with Christian, consenting "carelessly" to let Christian carry the dice with him. (After they have left we find that Diggory Venn has been sitting quietly concealed in the room. He soon goes out.) Of course Wildeve urges Christian to shake the dice for the money. They find a spot to sit and play by lantern light.

Wildeve wins it all, thinking it is Thomasin's anyway. Christian, in his agony, blurts out that half was for Clym. Wildeve remarks that "it would have been graceful" of Mrs. Yeobright "to have given them to his wife Eustacia." As they part, Christian to totter home, Wildeve ready to return to the inn, "a figure rose from behind a neighboring bush and came forward into the lantern light. It was the reddleman approaching."

Comment

In this chapter, we have the bare forces of good and evil at work. Diggory Venn, the good man, is present, though invisible, to overhear incidents which he uses to advantage in behalf of Thomasin. Wildeve, the evil man, carries forward a situation, which began in jest, to a revengeful conclusion against Mrs. Yeobright, who has so often wounded his pride.

CHAPTER 8: A NEW FORCE DISTURBS THE CURRENT

Wildeve stares at the reddleman. Venn coolly admits eavesdropping and challenges Wildeve to play with him for the money not his own. Wildeve haughtily replies, "It is my own. It is my wife's and what is hers is mine." They play feverishly till Diggory Venn wins all the guineas away from Wildeve Thomasin's and Clym's. (Diggory believes them all to be Thomasin's.) At one time Wildeve is so furious, he seizes the dice and hurls them into the bushes; they retrieve only one, but still go on playing. A moth flies into the lantern and extinguishes it. Having no matches, Wildeve gathers thirteen glowworms and ranges them on a rock for light. Thus they play on till Wildeve has no more money. Venn gathers up the stakes and withdraws. Wildeve sits stupefied, then finally gets up and walks toward the inn. He hears a carriage approaching, and by the carriage lamps sees Eustacia and Clym, who are driving to their new home. All Wildeve's passion for Eustacia is rekindled at the sight of her sitting with another man's arm around her waist. Further along the road, Diggory Venn stops the carriage and 'inquires for Mrs. Wildeve. They tell him she will be along soon. He waits nearly half an hour before Thomasin comes in a vehicle driven by Charley. Stopping them, the reddleman gives Mrs. Wildeve the parcel of the hundred guineas, telling her it is from Mrs. Yeobright.

Comment

Here we see Wildeve make a fool of Christian; and then we are pleased to see Diggory Venn make a fool of Wildeve, actually taunting Wildeve with the very words he had used in leading Christian on previously. Book Third ends with a **foreshadowing** of events to come: "It had not been comprehended by the reddleman that half-way through the performance the game was continued with the money of another person; and it was an error which afterward helped to cause more misfortune than treble the loss in money value could have done."

Summary: The plot now becomes ever more melodramatic as Hardy uses Mrs. Yeobright's great bitterness toward Eustacia and Wildeve, Wildeve's compelling desire for revenge, and Eustacia's dramatic passion for life - to show how the bad passions of people can influence the lives of good, reasonable individuals like Clym and Thomasin.

1. Clym Yeobright is revealed as a thoughtful young man, bent on fitting into his right niche in life. He will give up the diamond business and live at home as a teacher.

2.   Clym reveals his plan to his mother, who disapproves. He schemes to see Eustacia Vye.

3.   Clym meets Eustacia and falls in love. He and his mother become estranged by his determination to marry Eustacia.

4.   Eustacia accepts Clym's proposal.

5.   Mrs. Yeobright hears of the engagement and speaks harshly to Clym. He goes to Eustacia. They agree to marry in two weeks.

6.   Clym packs his things and leaves his mother's house. He rents a small cottage about five miles away and moves in. The wedding day is to be June twenty-fifth. Mrs. Yeobright is inconsolable; she tells Thomasin of the guineas she has to divide between Thomasin and Clym.

7.   The wedding takes place. Mrs. Yeobright entrusts Christian with the guineas to take to Thomasin and Clym. He loses them to Wildeve in a dice game.

8.   Diggory Venn wins the guineas back from Wildeve and presents them to Thomasin from her aunt, believing they are all hers.

THE RETURN OF THE NATIVE

BOOK FOURTH: THE CLOSED DOOR

. . . .

CHAPTER 1: THE RENCOUNTER BY THE POOL

The month of July is a honeymoon for Clym and Eustacia. They live in their little house at Alderworth "with a monotony which" is "delightful to them." If it rains, they are happy because they can "remain indoors together all day"; if it is sunny, they are charmed because they can "sit together on the hills." After three or four weeks, however, Clym resumes his reading. Eustacia ponders on how she shall get Clym to go to Paris. Her hopes are "bound up in this dream," but so far she has never dared to bring up the subject. Early in August an incident occurs that helps bring matters to ahead. Soon after receipt of her aunt's money, Thomasin had sent a note to thank her; but Mrs. Yeobright has never heard from Clym. Wondering, she questions Christian and gets confused replies. Hearing that Eustacia is visiting her grandfather, Mrs. Yeobright decides to go to see her and find out. When Christian learns her intent, he blurts out the truth as far as he knows it - "that the guineas had been won by Wildeve." He tells Mrs. Yeobright that

Wildeve had said "you ought to have gied Mr. Clym's share to Eustacia, and that's perhaps what he'll do himself."

The thought of this is "as irritating a pain as any that Mrs. Yeobright" has ever borne. She starts off to Mistover. Eustacia is standing by the pool. Mrs. Yeobright immediately asks, "Have you received a gift from Thomasin's husband?" Eustacia fires up "all too quickly." "Money from Mr. Wildeve? No-never! Madam, what do you mean by that?" Eustacia accuses Mrs. Yeobright of always having been against her. Mrs. Yeobright says that she has simply been for Clym, and Eustacia resents the implication that Clym needed guarding against her. She says, "It was a condescension in me to be Clym's wife and not a maneuver." Mrs. Yeobright counters with "I have never heard anything to show that my son's lineage is not as good as the Vyes' - perhaps better." Eustacia, beside herself, explodes: "If I had known ... what I know now, that I would be living in this wild heath a month after my marriage, I - I should have thought twice before agreeing." More angry words are spoken. Eustacia finally says, "Will you go away from me? You are no friend!" Mrs. Yeobright's parting words are: "Only show my son one-half the temper you have shown me today - and you will find that though he is as gentle as a child with you now, he can be as hard as steel!"

Comment

Here we have two hot-tempered, self-pitying women, one on the offensive, the other on the defensive. The resulting clash greatly widens the breach between Clym's mother and his wife, advancing the plot considerably toward its **climax**. The fact, revealed later, that Clym's mother has a weak heart may make this encounter a real contribution to her death.

CHAPTER 2: HE IS SET UPON BY ADVERSITIES BUT HE SINGS A SONG

Eustacia hurries home to Clym, flushed and excited. She tells him: "I have seen your mother; and I will never see her again!" Clym is confused, but he believes there must be some mistake about the implication that Wildeve has given Eustacia money. Eustacia, beside herself, blurts out, "take me to Paris, and go on with your old occupation, Clym!" Clym explains that he has completely given up that idea and thought Eustacia knew it, but Eustacia reveals that she has been hoping constantly that he will change his mind. Clym is disconcerted at being confronted by "the fact of the indirectness of a woman's movement toward her desire." He is firm in his resolve to stay on the heath.

The next day Thomasin comes to deliver his share of guineas into Clym's hand. They speak together of the quarrel between Mrs. Yeobright and Eustacia. Clym believes that two people with such "inflammable natures" will never be friends. He redoubles his efforts at studying so that he may make "a show of progress in his scholastic plans"; soon he suffers serious eyestrain and is forced to give up all reading for many weeks. One day, despondent, he meets Humphrey, the furze-cutter, on the heath. Humphrey, expressing concern for Clym's condition, says, "Now if yours was a low-class work like mine, you could go on with it just the same." Clym is struck by the idea. Thinking about it all the way home, he tells Eustacia he is going to be a furze- and turf-cutter. Bitter tears, which he cannot see, roll down Eustacia's face. The next way he borrows proper clothing and goes forth with Humphrey.

Day after day he now works from four in the morning till noon, sleeping for an hour or two in the afternoon, and working again till nine at night. The monotony of his work soothes him. Often he sings to himself. Eustacia finds him thus one day, working on the heath and singing happily. "The proud fair woman bowed her head and wept in sick despair at thought of the blasting effect upon her own life" of Clym's lack of rebellion against his "social failure." "I would rather starve than do it!... And you can sing!" They talk earnestly and heatedly about each other's faults. Clym finally touches her arm and says, "Now don't you suppose ... that I cannot rebel ... as well as you.... But the more I see of life the more I perceive that there is nothing particularly great in its greatest walks, and therefore nothing particularly small in mine of furze-cutting."

Comment

We now see how different are Clym's and Eustacia's natures. Clym under misfortune and disappointment finds a way to be happy and useful. Eustacia cannot take disappointment and begins to wilt. Her fanciful hopes can no longer sustain her. She broods and sulks and bemoans her lot. Here is an essential part of Hardy's philosophy (as presented in this novel): Our reason can help us surmount the difficulties of environment and blind instinct - if we will let it.

CHAPTER 3: SHE GOES OUT TO BATTLE AGAINST DEPRESSION

It is near the end of August. Clym and Eustacia are having their early dinner together, she forlorn and discouraged, he cheerful and comforting: "Come, brighten up, dearest; we shall be all right again.... I solemnly promise I'll leave off cutting furze as soon as I have the power to do anything better." Eustacia refuses to be comforted. She asks if she may go to the gipsying (village picnic) at East Egdon this afternoon. Clym consents, hoping this will raise her spirits.

She dresses with great care and sets forth about five o'clock. Nearing the picnic grounds she hears the band, then sees the dancing and the tables where the "elderly dames" prepare tea. She watches from a distance, then walks along a little farther, hoping to see someone she knows. As dusk comes on, she dares to advance a little closer without fear of being recognized. As she watches the whirling dancers, she hears her name whispered over her shoulder. It is Wildeve. He asks Eustacia to dance with him, telling her she can pull down her veil and not be recognized. She consents. Wildeve is "in a delirium of exquisite misery. To clasp as his for five minutes what was another man's through all the rest of the year was a kind of thing he of all men could appreciate." After three dances, they sit down on the grass together. He sympathizes with her lot, and adds to her despair and humiliation by saying he was surprised to hear her husband had taken a cottage. "I thought ... he would have taken you off to a home in Paris.... He will, I suppose, return there with you, if his sight gets strong again?" She is almost weeping. He offers to walk home with her. They set forth, he helping her over the rough spots. As they approach Throope Corner (near Clym's cottage) they see Clym and Diggory Venn coming toward them. Wildeve bids Eustacia goodnight and disappears.

She meets Clym, and Diggory walks on quickly by a short cut to the Quiet Woman Inn. He has seen a man leave Eustacia's side, and is determined to find out if it was Wildeve. He learns from Thomasin that her husband has not yet returned from his horse buying. Asking if Wildeve was wearing "a white wideawake" (a broad-brimmed felt hat) Diggory tells Thomasin that he saw him at Throope Corner leading home "a beauty with a white face and a mane as black as night." Thomasin wishes Diggory could tell her some secret to keep her husband at home evenings.

When Wildeve arrives, Venn has gone. Thomasin asks about the horse. Wildeve says he has not bought one. Thomasin tells him the reddleman has told her of the beauty he saw Wildeve leading home. Wildeve says it must have been someone else; but he perceives "that Venn's counter-moves have begun again." (We can almost hear him utter frustrated curses directed at Diggory's meddlesome interference.)

Comment

Eustacia seeks outside diversion and so meets with temptation. Diggory Venn reappears as the guardian of Thomasin's happiness and as Wildeve's opponent. An interesting description of another country custom, "a gipsying" is given here. "One of the lawn-like oases" on the heath is chosen for the village festivity. "The lusty notes of the East Egdon band" are heard from the musicians "sitting in a blue wagon with red wheels scrubbed as bright as new, and arched with sticks, to which boughs and flowers were tied." There was a "grand central dance of fifteen or twenty couples, flanked by minor dances of interior individuals ... not always in strict keeping with the tune." The older women prepare tea at a table near the fire. "A whole village-full of sensuous emotion, scattered abroad all the year long, surged here in a focus for an hour."

CHAPTER 4: ROUGH COERCION IS EMPLOYED

Diggory Venn is impressed by Thomasin's plea: "Help me to keep him at home in the evenings." He must maneuver on Thomasin's behalf. When Wildeve wanders in the direction of Clym's cottage in the evening, he trips and falls headlong. Investigating, he finds some tufts of grass tied together by a cord of reddish color. He believes that the reddleman and Mrs. Yeobright are in league against him. His eagerness for intrigue heightened, he goes again to Clym's cottage and sends a moth in the window to flutter around Eustacia's candle. She recognizes this as their old signal. She intends to slip out to meet Wildeve; but just then a loud knocking sounds on the door. Clym insists on going to the door himself. No one is there. Wildeve realizes that Diggory Venn has outwitted him constable is away, and cooling down, Wildeve goes on home. He decides again. As Wildeve is walking home, he is shot at from the bushes. Aroused now, he goes to the constable's house to get help. But to visit Eustacia by day. Meanwhile Diggory goes to see Mrs. Yeobright. He tells her about Wildeve's attempts to see Eustacia, and persuades her that she should go to see the afflicted Clym. At the same time, Clym is persuading Eustacia that they must forget the past and do all they can to welcome his mother to their home.

Comment

Diggory Venn, always the hero fencing with Wildeve the opponent, is astonishing in his elfish ways of harassing the adversary and thwarting his plans.

CHAPTER 5: THE JOURNEY ACROSS THE HEATH

On August thirty-first Mrs. Yeobright starts out on a hot morning walk across the heath toward her son's house five miles away. Never having been there, she takes a few wrong paths, and finally, seeing a man at work, asks directions. He tells her to follow "that furze-cutter, ma'am, going up that footpath yond." She does as directed, and begins to recognize the gait of the man ahead. It is her son. She sees him go into his house. It is difficult for her to accept that Clym has actually become a furze-cutter. She feels "agitated, weary, and unwell," and sits down under the shade of fir trees to recover her spirits. As she rests she sees a second man approaching the gate and going in. At first she is annoyed to have her visit so interrupted, but then she decides it may be easier to have a third party present. She walks down the hill to the gate and looks into the garden, preparing to enter.

Comment

In Book First we had a penetrating description of Egdon Heath in November. Now we are given an equally penetrating description of the heath on a hot August day. "The sun had branded the whole heath with his mark, even the purple heath-flowers having put on a brownness under the dry blazes of the few preceding days ... the air around" pulsated "silently ... oppressing the earth with lassitude.... All the shallower ponds had decreased to a vaporous mud amid which the maggoty shapes of innumerable obscene creatures could be distinctly seen heaving and wallowing with enjoyment."

CHAPTER 6: A CONJUNCTURE AND ITS RESULT UPON THE PEDESTRIAN

It is Wildeve who has entered the house. Eustacia lets him in. Clym is sleeping soundly on the hearthrug. Eustacia and Wildeve talk about the past, and Wildeve declares his constant love for Eustacia. Mrs. Yeobright knocks on the door. Eustacia, having peered out the window to see who is there, fears to let her in. She takes Wildeve to the back. Having heard Clym stir and mutter the word "mother," she assumes he is going to let Mrs. Yeobright in. Eustacia lets Wildeve out by the back door. Going inside again, she finds Clym still asleep, and Mrs. Yeobright gone from the door.

Mrs. Yeobright, knowing Clym to be inside, and having seen Eustacia peer out the window when she knocked, believes they have refused to let her in. She stumbles back along the path in the hot sun. Johnny Nunsuch catches up with her and keeps her company for a while, bringing her some tepid water to drink. Finally he tires of waiting while she rests and wants to go along home. She asks him to tell his mother that "you have seen a broken-hearted woman cast off by her son." Mrs. Yeobright, alone now, falters along about two-thirds of the way home till she has to sit down to rest on "a little patch of shepherd's thyme" which makes a "perfumed mat" on the path. She ceases to think about her own plight. Her thoughts descend "upon the roof of Clym's house."

Comment

Here is one of Hardy's most melodramatic scenes: the lovers plotting while the husband sleeps; the face at the window; the spurned mother. Continued description of the heath in August scorches us with intensity.

CHAPTER 7: THE TRAGIC MEETING OF TWO OLD FRIENDS

Meanwhile Clym has awakened. He sits up and tells Eustacia his bad dream: he had taken Eustacia to his mother's house; they could not get in, but heard her inside crying for help. His nightmare strengthens Clym's resolve to go to see his mother, and he decides to go at once. Eustacia tries to persuade him to wait till the next day, but he must go now. On the way, he discovers his mother lying by the path, barely alive. He picks her up and starts to carry her home. She cannot speak, and eventually becomes so restless that Clym takes her into a nearby shed, and, laying her on a bed of dry fern, runs to Timothy Fairway for help. Many of the heath people are congregated there, and they all run back with Clym. Mrs. Yeobright manages to indicate her swollen foot. They realize she has been bitten by an adder. Someone goes for the doctor, while others prepare a remedy. A fresh-killed adder is brought; a fire is built; the oil of the adder is fried out and applied to the wound.

Comment

Another country custom, the curing of an adder bite, is described here in detail. The chapter is rich in examples of the operation of "fate" (chance, or accident) upon the characters: Mrs. Yeobright's arrival at the same time as Wildeve; Clym's dream, with its astonishing similarity to the real facts; the adder bite (the heath again claiming a victim) which helps to bring about Mrs. Yeobright's death.

CHAPTER 8: EUSTACIA HEARS OF GOOD FORTUNE AND BEHOLDS EVIL

Eustacia, at home, prepares to walk out in the direction of Blooms-End to meet Clym coming back. Her grandfather drives up to tell her news of Wildeve's inheritance: a fortune of eleven thousand pounds from an uncle in Canada. She concludes Wildeve's visit in the morning was to tell her. "How much he wishes he had me now, that he might give me all I desire!" she thinks, as she walks along to meet Clym. She is "disturbed in her reverie by a voice behind." It is, of course, Wildeve. She congratulates him on his fortune. He tells her he means to travel; Thomasin may prefer to stay at home. As they wander along toward Blooms-End they see a light in a hut. Eustacia asks Wildeve to investigate, while she stands just outside peering in.

At this moment, Mrs. Yeobright is breathing her last breaths. The doctor attributes her death, not to the snake bite, but to exhaustion from a weak heart and a long walk in the heat. Johnny Nunsuch runs in to tell his mother, who is helping the dying woman, "That woman asleep there walked along with me today; and she said I was to say that I had seed her, and she was a broken-hearted woman and cast off by her son...." Eustacia, outside, hears Clym utter a "confused sob," but she dares not to go in. She and Wildeve withdraw back onto the heath. Eustacia says, "I am to blame for this. There is evil in store for me." "Was she not admitted to your house after all?" asks Wildeve. "No; and that's where it all lies!" Eustacia, beside herself, dismisses Wildeve and walks on toward her home.

Comment

Here is a good place to describe Eustacia's grandfather. Though kindly in an absent-minded sort of way, he is also very undiscerning and tactless. When he tells Eustacia about Wildeve's fortune, he remarks, "What a fool you were, Eustacia ... in not sticking to him when you had him" He goes on to say he "would have been hot and strong against it" but "Why didn't you stick to him?" Then he shows his kindness by offering assistance: "What's mine is yours, you know."

The death of Mrs. Yeobright is the crisis or turning point of the novel. Up to now, the plot has mounted; from now on, the fortunes of the main characters will decline. Mrs. Yeobright's death is frequently attributed to the adder's bite, but the doctor explains, quite explicitly: "She has suffered somewhat from the bite of the adder; but it is exhaustion which has overpowered her.... Her heart was previously affected, and physical exhaustion has dealt the finishing blow."

Summary: Book Fourth gives us action ever mounting to the crisis, which is the death of Clym's mother.

1.   Mrs. Yeobright goes to see Eustacia at Mistover. The two women quarrel and part with great bitterness.

2.   Having almost lost his eyesight, Clym finds peace of mind in becoming a furze-cutter. Eustacia is crushed and humiliated by his occupation.

3.   Eustacia goes to the village picnic and dances with Wildeve. Diggory Venn sees Wildeve bringing her home.

4.   Diggory Venn employs simple but effective means to thwart Wildeve's attempts to see Eustacia. Venn goes to Mrs. Yeobright to urge her to visit her son, while Clym urges Eustacia to welcome his mother if she comes to see them.

5.   Mrs. Yeobright sets forth to visit Clym.

6.   Eustacia, thinking Clym has awakened to do it, and shielding herself and Wildeve, does not answer Mrs. Yeobright's knock. Mrs. Yeobright staggers back over the heath, thinking she has been cast out.

7.   Clym, waking from a bad dream, determines to visit his mother immediately. He finds her unconscious as he walks over the heath.

8.   Mrs. Yeobright dies of exhaustion. Johnny Nunsuch reports her last words: that she has been cast out by her son.

THE RETURN OF THE NATIVE

BOOK FIFTH: THE DISCOVERY

. . . .

CHAPTER 1: "WHEREFORE IS LIGHT GIVEN TO HIM THAT IS IN MISERY?"

It is now three weeks after Mrs. Yeobright's funeral. Clym has been ill and out of his mind with grief and self-blame. Eustacia is caring for him. He keeps repeating, "If she had only come to see me! I longed that she would." Eustacia cannot bring herself to tell him that his mother did come. A little later in the evening, Thomasin comes to see them. Clym renews his tragic regrets, finally saying, "Do you think, Thomasin, that she knew me - that she did not die in that horrid mistaken notion about my not forgiving her, which I can't tell you how she acquired?" Thomasin reassures him. Eustacia says nothing. "Why didn't she come to my house? I would have taken her in and showed her how much I loved her...." Still Eustacia says nothing. Clym feels it would be better for all if he died, too. Thomasin tries to soothe him. Wildeve drives over to get his wife, and Eustacia slips down to speak to him. She admits that she has not told

Clym of his mother's visit. Wildeve advises her to tell Clym, but "You must only tell part - for his own sake." "What part should I keep back?" Wildeve replies, "That I was in the house at the time." Eustacia agrees. Thomasin comes down, and she and her husband drive away.

Comment

Here Eustacia tries to reason Clym out of his dreadful remorse and sorrow for his mother. He is as impossible to reason with as Eustacia was, when Clym tried to get her to accept his furze-cutting. Eustacia dares not speak the words that will ease Clym's soul.

CHAPTER 2: A LURID LIGHT BREAKS IN UPON A DARKENED UNDERSTANDING

It is now October, and Clym is able to be up and walking in his garden. One evening Christian appears to tell Clym that "Mrs. Wildeve is doing well of a girl" which was born at noon. Clym is glad to hear that Thomasin has her baby and all is well. He asks Christian if he saw Clym's mother the day before she died." Christian replies, "No.... But I zeed her the morning of the same day she died." He reveals that Mrs. Yeobright had told him she was going to see Clym, excited, asks if Christian knows why. Christian says he does not, but that Diggory, the reddleman, must know. "He called upon her and sat with her the evening before she set out to see you." Clym sends Christian to find Venn. Meanwhile, Clym goes to his mother's house to look over its contents. While he is there, Diggory Venn appears, asking for Mrs. Yeobright. Clym tells him the news. Diggory explains his talk with Mrs. Yeobright. He stoutly maintains that she had forgiven Clym and forgiven his wife, and was going to see them to make friends. Clym is greatly puzzled by this contradiction. He decides to go to talk with Johnny Nunsuch. Johnny repeats exactly what he said before, but when Clym asks, "She was going to Alderworth when you first met her?" Johnny replies, "No; she was coming away." Clym tries to change his story, but Johnny is firm. He tells how he saw Clym's mother at Clym's house; that she sat under the trees and "looked at a man who came up and went into your house...." The poor lady went and knocked at your door, and the lady with the black hair looked out of the side window at her.... And when she saw the young lady look out of the window the old lady knocked again; and ... nobody came." He tells how Mrs. Yeobright came away, breathing hard, and how they met and walked together till she sent Johnny home. Clym believes now that Eustacia cast off his mother, letting Mrs. Yeobright think it was he who did not answer the knock.

Comment

Johnny Nunsuch explodes the whole plot right in Clym's face. Clym now can think only the worst of Eustacia. A subordinate, but important, part of this chapter is the mention of Susan Nunsuch, who still believes that Eustacia is bewitching her ailing Johnny. Susan's power of imagination is strong and casts an evil spell over Eustacia, thus fortifying and combining Hardy's beliefs in the compelling power of the mind over the body and the influence of the brooding forces of fate.

CHAPTER 3: EUSTACIA DRESSES HERSELF ON A BLACK MORNING

Clym returns home and goes straight to his wife's room. His face is "ashy, haggard, and terrible." He demands, "Tell me, now, where is he who was with you on the afternoon of the thirty-first of August? Under the bed? Up the chimney?" She replies that she does not remember dates so exactly. He answers harshly, "The day I mean was the day you shut the door against my mother and killed her ... you looked out of the window upon her - you had a man in the house with you - you sent her away to die ... confess every word!" Eustacia's pride is aroused. "Never! I'll hold my tongue like the very death that I don't mind meeting, even though I can clear myself of half you believe by speaking." He presses her to admit the man was Thomasin's husband. She will neither admit nor defend herself. Instead, she accuses him of wronging her, "All persons of refinement have been scared away from me since I sank into the mire of marriage .... You deceived me - not by words, but by appearances." She finally breaks into tears, confessing she did not open the door the first time but would have answered the second knock, except for thinking he had gone to the door himself. By the time she realized he had not opened it, his mother was gone. She adds that "Now I will leave you - forever and ever!" He replies that he may be able to find pity for her if she reveals the man's identity. She flings her shawl around her and goes out. Not long after, someone comes from the Wildeves' to say that the baby has been named Eustacia Clementine. "What mockery!" cries Clym, "This unhappy marriage of mine to be perpetuated in that child's name!"

Comment

Here is great melodrama. Clym almost becomes villainous as he bullies and hounds Eustacia to confess. Out of his mind with rage and grief and disillusionment, he smashes open her desk and tears open her letters. He commands her to "Tell all." She proudly refuses and leaves his house.

CHAPTER 4: THE MINISTRATIONS OF A HALF-FORGOTTEN ONE

Eustacia stumbles toward Mistover. She finds the house locked, but she discovers Charley in the stable. He tells her that Captain Vye will not be back until evening. Charley, realizing she feels sick at heart, offers to climb in a window and let her in the door. He assists her into the room and to the sofa. He builds a fire for her and brings food, holding tea to her lips for her to sip. He stays around unobtrusively while she dozes and gets her strength back. When she goes upstairs to her room, he follows to assist her. She looks in at her grandfather's brace of pistols hanging near the head of his bed. When later she goes back to get one to end her life, they are gone. Charley admits he has locked them away. "I saw you looking at them too long." He refuses to give them to her, but he promises not to say anything about her wanting them, "if you promise not to think of it again." She tell, him, "You need not fear. The moment has passed." When her grandfather returns, he has her old room ready for her, and asks no questions.

Comment

We see now that Eustacia has three men who care for her: Clym, Wildeve, and the lowly Charley. These three match Thomasin's three lovers: Clym as a lad, Wildeve, and the lowly Diggory Venn. Wildeve is the fascinator, common to both; the others, though prosaic, are the staunch loyal ones.

CHAPTER 5: AN OLD MOVE INADVERTENTLY REPEATED

For a week Eustacia does not leave her grandfather's house. Charley, hoping she will remain at Mistover, tries to keep her amused by bringing all sorts of pleasant distractions from the heath, and leaving them where she will be sure to see them. There are such delights as white trumpet-shaped mosses, red-headed lichens, stone arrow-heads, and faceted crystals. One day Eustacia ventures outside with her grandfather's telescope. As she sweeps it round the heath, she sees a wagon moving toward Blooms-End. It is filled with her furniture. She realizes Clym is moving to his mother's cottage. Another day she sees Thomasin carrying her baby for a walk upon the heath. The fifth of November is again coming around. Charley plans a surprise for Eustacia: He builds a bonfire. She is pleased and goes out to thank him. As the fire dies down, Charley moves away, but Eustacia still stands by the bank. She is startled to hear a splash and then a second splash. Wildeve appears. Eustacia quickly tells him she did not light the fire. Wildeve sympathizes with her plight, and Eustacia weeps. Wildeve offers to assist her to get away. She says if he can help her get to Budmouth, she can manage to get to Paris from there herself. But she is not sure she should accept his help. "If I wish to go and decide to accept your company, I will signal to you some evening at eight o'clock punctually, and this will mean that you are to be ready with a horse and trap at twelve o'clock the same night." Wildeve promises to look every night for her signal.

Comment

How Eustacia loves melodramatic romance: signals and royal commands. Faithful, loving Charley has unwittingly become the means of bringing Eustacia to her untimely end. He, with his surprise bonfire, starts the chain of events that leads to catastrophe.

CHAPTER 6: THOMASIN ARGUES WITH HER COUSIN AND HE WRITES A LETTER

Clym is now living at Blooms-End, hoping that Eustacia will come to him. On the night of November fifth, he goes to see Thomasin and her husband, thinking that he may lead Wildeve to saying "something to reveal the extent to which Eustacia was compromised." Of course Wildeve is not at home. Thomasin greets Clym gladly. She is shocked at what he tells her of Eustacia and his mother, but she urges him to make up. "Believe her sorry, and send for her." When Clym reaches home again he sits down and writes Eustacia a letter, saying that his heart wants her back, no matter what his reason tells him. If she will return, she will be warmly welcomed. He plans to send the letter the next night, if she has not come.

When Wildeve returns to the inn, Thomasin asks where he has been, saying, "I don't like your vanishing so in the evenings." She admits she has heard rumors that he is seeing Eustacia. Not admitting anything, Wildeve, seeing "her eyes … brimming with tears," consoles her the best he can, and no more is said.

Comment

Often Hardy's plot turns on someone's delayed action. Here it is Clym's decision not to send the letter till the next evening that contributes to the chain of events.

CHAPTER 7: THE NIGHT OF THE SIXTH OF NOVEMBER

Eustacia, meanwhile, hopes constantly that Clym will come to get her. But on the afternoon of the sixth of November, deciding that this is a vain hope, she packs a few things into a bundle suitable for her to carry. Then she goes out to take a walk on the heath. She passes Susan Nunsuch's house. Mrs. Nunsuch sees her and shakes her fist at her as she disappears down the path. Returning home, Eustacia lights a torch of furze at precisely eight o'clock. She sees a similar light flare-up in the vicinity of the inn. She goes in and has supper with her grandfather, then retires early to sit in her dark bedroom till time to leave. As Captain Vye is sitting by the fire alone downstairs, a knock on the door reveals Timothy Fairway with Clym's letter to Eustacia. Captain Vye takes it upstairs, but, seeing no light under Eustacia's door, brings it down again and puts it upon the mantelpiece. He goes to bed about eleven. Just as he lies down, he sees a flash of light on the flagpole. He realizes that Eustacia has turned on her light. He gets up to tell her of the letter, but finds she has left the house.

When Eustacia goes outside, she discovers it is raining. Wrapping her cloak tightly around her, she goes on just the same. But she pauses on Rainbarrow to think. "A sudden recollection had flashed on her this moment: she had not money enough for undertaking a long journey." She speaks her agony aloud: "How I have tried and tried to be a splendid woman, and how destiny has been against me! … I do not deserve my lot!" She feels that

Wildeve is "not great enough" for her to break her marriage vow for him - and she has not money enough to go alone.

Susan Nunsuch is busy in her home making a wax effigy of Eustacia, sticking pins in it, and burning it. She feels little Johnny is ill because Eustacia has bewitched him. She uses her superstition to cast off the spell.

Comment

Hardy tantalizes us with near-misses. Not only did Clym delay in sending the letter, but also, when the letter arrives just in the nick of time, Captain Vye blunders twice in not delivering the letter to Eustacia. We feel that Eustacia is right: Destiny is against her.

There is a careful description here of the superstition of the wax effigy. Susan Nunsuch softens beeswax; kneads the pieces into a woman's form; dresses the figure in a red ribbon and inks in sandal-shoes; as a finishing touch she ties a black thread on the head as a riband. Then she takes a paper of pins and, one by one, thrusts them into all parts of the waxen body. Next, holding the wax image in tongs over the fire, she lets it melt away, while she recites the Lord's Prayer backward.

CHAPTER 8: RAIN, DARKNESS, AND ANXIOUS, WANDERERS

This sixth of November is "one of those nights when cracks in the walls of old churches widen, when ancient stains on the ceilings of decayed manor-houses are renewed and enlarged from the size of a man's hand to an area of many feet." Clym paces around his house restively, thinking of Eustacia, hoping she will come as soon as she receives his letter. There is a knock at the door, but it is only Thomasin and her baby. Thomasin believes her husband is going to leave her. She tells Clym of Wildeve's preparing to go on a journey tonight; he has said he will be back "tomorrow," but she knows he is taking a large sum of money. She believes he may be taking Eustacia. She asks Clym to go and persuade Wildeve not to leave. Clym is just about to go out when Captain Vye knocks at the door, asking for his granddaughter. Clym tells him she may be about to elope with Wildeve. Captain Vye hopes it is no worse than elopement. Clym says, "Worse? What's worse than the worst a wife can do?" Captain Vye tells him then of the pistols, and why Charley had hidden them. Clym starts off to see Wildeve, asking Captain Vye to accompany him. The captain, however, feels his legs will carry him no farther now than his own house: "If they are interrupted in their flight, she will be sure to come back to me, and I ought to be at home ...."

Thomasin cannot endure being in Clym's house alone for long. She wraps the baby up warmly again and starts back in the rain. She has no fears of the heath, but the wet ferns drench her skirts and the wind blows her about. She comes upon Diggory Venn's wagon. The door is open. She is about to venture in to sit by the fire, when Diggory returns, saying, "I thought you went down the slope. How do you come back here again?" It seems that another woman went by, just before she came. Thinking it must be Eustacia going to meet Wildeve, Thomasin tells Diggory she must go at once. He accompanies her and carries the baby. Through the rain, they can see a light which Thomasin thinks is from the window of the Quiet Woman Inn. Diggory tells her that the light is not at the inn, but below it, across the marsh. Thomasin urges him to lead her toward the light.

Comment

As the **climax** approaches, the plot becomes more melodramatic. Here Thomasin, the deserted mother, wanders over the storm-tossed heath most of the night with her baby in her arms. First she goes to Clym; then she goes to Diggory; then she and Diggory stagger together over the drenched heath toward the light across the marsh. They believe "the other woman" has slipped past them on her way to the rendezvous.

CHAPTER 9: SIGHTS AND SOUNDS DRAW THE WANDERERS TOGETHER

Wildeve, having seen Eustacia's signal, has prepared for the journey. At twenty minutes to twelve, he goes to the stable, lights the lamps of the carriage, and leads the horse out to a spot about a quarter of a mile below the inn. Here he waits, sheltered by a high bank. The blustering wind drives the rain slantwise. "One sound rose above this din of weather ... the roaring of" Shadwater Weir (a weir is a dam) on the river near the road. Wildeve wonders if Eustacia will come in such weather: "Poor thing; 'tis like her ill-luck." Shortly he hears footsteps. Clym Yeobright appears in the lamp-light. Wildeve stays unseen in the shadow, hoping Clym will pass by. Just then they both hear "a dull sound ... the fall of a body into the stream." Clym starts at the sound. "Good God! can it be she?" Wildeve, equally startled, forgets to remain hidden and blurts out, "Why should it be she?" Yeobright echoes, "Why should it be she? Because last week she would have put an end to her life if she had been able.... Take one of the lamps and come with me."

The two men hurry to the dam bridge, and Clym shines his lamp down upon the waters. They see a dark, floating body in a back current; the agonized Wildeve leaps into the stream without removing his overcoat. Clym places the lamp upright against a post and runs around to a lower part of the pool where he can wade in. Reaching deep water, he swims to where he can see Wildeve struggling.

Diggory Venn and Thomasin, meanwhile, seeing the lamp moving toward the dam, follow its course. Venn hands the baby to Thomasin, telling her to run home and get the stable lad to rouse any men he can to come to help. Diggory, finding a board, wades into the lower part of the pool with his lantern in his hand. In deep water he can float on the plank. He propels himself around, holding the lantern aloft, and at first sees "a woman's bonnet floating alone." Then a man comes to the surface almost beside him. Diggory puts "the ring of the lantern between his teeth" and, seizing the man by the collar, pushes his way back to shallow water by means of the plank. When he drags the man out on the bank, he finds another man clinging to his legs. At this moment, two men come running to help him lift and lay "the apparently drowned persons ... upon the grass.... Venn turned the light upon their faces. The one who had been uppermost was Yeobright; he who had been completely submerged was Wildeve." Venn tells the men they must search the water again for a woman. They tear handrails off the bridge and begin to probe the pool. When something moves against their thrust, Venn vanishes under the water and comes up "with an armful of wet drapery enclosing a woman's cold form" - all that remains of "the desperate Eustacia."

The men carry the bodies to the carriage, and take them thus to the inn. A doctor is sent for; "the insensible forms of Eustacia, Clym, and Wildeve" are laid near the fire and "such restorative processes as could be thought of were adopted." Thomasin applies a bottle of hartshorn (ammonia) to the nostrils of each victim. Clym sighs and soon breathes distinctly, but neither of the others can be revived.

When the doctor arrives, Diggory Venn feels he is no longer needed and ought to leave. He crosses the heath back to his van, changes to dry clothes, and lies down. But he cannot sleep. He must return to help Thomasin bear her grief. Back at the inn, Olly Dowden and another woman are bustling around the kitchen. They tell Diggory that "Mr. Yeobright is better; but Mrs. Yeobright and Mr. Wildeve are dead and cold." Answering his question about Thomasin they say, "She is as well as can be expected. The doctor had her put between blankets, for she was almost as wet as they that had been in the river." They invite him to sit by the fire, telling him "Mis'ess says you be to have whatever you want, and she was sorry when she was told that you'd gone away." As Diggory sits thinking of happier occasions at that fire, the nurse comes downstairs with a roll of soggy paper. She strings a line across the fire irons and pins banknotes one by one on the line to dry out. "Poor master's banknotes.... They were found in his pocket...." The doctor comes down finally and drives away.

About four o'clock in the morning, Charley, sent by Captain Vye, comes knocking at the door. Diggory tells him the news. "Charley's only utterance was a feeble, indistinct sound. He stood quite still; then he burst out spasmodically, 'I shall see her once more?' A voice behind him says, "You shall." It is Clym, wrapped in a blanket and looking like a ghost. All three go upstairs. Eustacia, lying still in death, looks stately and dignified; "the expression of her finely carved mouth was pleasant ... her black hair surrounded her brow like a forest." Her complexion had a youthful glow "more than whiteness; it was almost light." Wildeve has less repose in his face, "but the same luminous youthfulness overspread it." When the three men leave the room, Clym speaks. "She is the second woman I have killed this year. I was a great cause of my mother's death; and I am the chief cause of hers … my great regret is that for what I have done no man or law can punish me!"

Comment

Hardy intended this to be the end of the novel, and artistically it is. The book was published serially, however, and readers demanded additional installments. They wanted Diggory Venn's devotion to be rewarded. Hardy himself considered Clym Yeobright the hero of the novel, but there are reasons why Diggory Venn might contest him for the role. Certainly many of the turns of events hinge on Diggory's decisive actions.

Summary: Everything now leads to the downfall of the characters ruled mainly by their instinctive passions. The deaths of Eustacia and Wildeve mark the end of the passionate action that overwhelms reason.

1.   Clym grieves night and day, not understanding why his mother died thinking he had cast her off.

2.   Clym learns that his mother had forgiven him and had come to see him, but was turned away from the door.

3.   Clym accuses Eustacia. She leaves Clym's house.

4.   Eustacia goes to Mistover and is cared for solicitously by Charley.

5.   Charley builds a November fifth bonfire, thus summoning Wildeve. Wildeve and Eustacia plan to escape.

6.   Thomasin urges Clym to make up with Eustacia. He writes her a warm, loving letter, but delays in sending it.

7.   Eustacia, not having received Clym's letter, goes to meet Wildeve.

8.   Thomasin warns Clym of a possible elopement. He goes to stop it. Thomasin also tells Diggory Venn, who goes too.

9.   Eustacia, realizing she has no money to get to Paris by herself, wanders despondently over the heath in the dark and is drowned. Clym and Wildeve go to her rescue, but it is Diggory Venn who drags all three from the water. Eustacia and Wildeve are past resuscitation, but Clym is revived.

Hardy has finished his novel's cycle with the rounding out of a complete year-November to November. This is the end of his story. But his readers demand a sequel, so the author obliges with Book Sixth.

THE RETURN OF THE NATIVE

BOOK SIXTH: AFTERCOURSES

. . . .

CHAPTER 1: THE INEVITABLE MOVEMENT ONWARD

For Eustacia and Wildeve, "misfortune had struck them gracefully, cutting off their erratic histories with a catastrophic dash, instead of ... long years of wrinkles, neglect, and decay," For Thomasin, "Vague misgivings about her future as a deserted wife were at an end." She busied herself with caring for her little Eustacia. "The spring came and calmed her; the summer came and soothed her; the autumn arrived, and she began to be comforted, for her little girl was strong and happy." Clym invited her to live at Blooms-End, and she accepted. He kept two rooms for himself "at the top of the back staircase." For Clym, "It might have been said that he had a wrinkled mind ... he could get nobody to reproach him, which was why he so bitterly reproached himself." His eyes improved; he often pored "over books of exceptionally large type." He took long walks on the heath.

One day, over a year after the tragedy, Diggory Venn comes to call. He now owns a dairy farm and is a handsome man, showing no signs of his former reddle trade. Thomasin is quite struck by his good looks. He has come to ask if a Maypole may be put up outside their fence. Thomasin is delighted that the May revel is to be so near. On the day, she dresses in her best; but Clym leaves the house and does not come back until the dancing is over. When he returns, Thomasin calls his attention to one man who is left strolling around the Maypole: It is Mr. Venn. At Clym's suggestion, she invites him in. Diggory politely declines, saying he is waiting for the moon to rise, so that he can "look for a glove dropped by one of the maidens." Thomasin sees him when he finds the glove: he raises it to his lips, then puts it into the pocket nearest his heart.

Comment

Although we know that Diggory Venn must win Thomasin eventually, Hardy deftly keeps us in suspense as to how this is to come about. In this chapter there is a lively description of another country custom: the Maypoling. The Maypole is decorated by the maidens of the village: "at the top of the pole were crossed hoops decked with small flowers; beneath these came a milkwhite zone of Maybloom; then a zone of bluebells, then of cowslips, then of lilacs, then of ragged-robin, daffodils, and so on, till the lowest stage was reached." This picture shows us alternating colors on the pole, of white, blue, yellow, lavender, red, yellow, and so on. Thomasin dresses in her best for the May revel, but she does not attend. Clym wonders if she is dressing up for him, but he does not feel that he can ever marry again.

CHAPTER 2: THOMASIN WALKS IN A GREEN PLACE BY THE ROMAN ROAD

Thomasin keeps wondering who the girl can be that has won Diggory Venn's heart. One afternoon she notices that one of her new gloves is missing. She asks Rachel, the baby's thirteen-year-old nurse, if she knows about it, and Rachel admits having taken the gloves to the Maypole and lost one. "Somebody gave me some money to buy another pair for you, but I have not been able to go anywhere to get 'em." "Who's somebody?" "Mr. Venn." "Did he know it was my glove?" "Yes. I told him." So now Thomasin knows. The next day she takes little Eustacia for a romp on the heath; Diggory Venn comes by on horseback, and Thomasin greets him with "Diggory, give me my glove." He does, and they talk. He tells her he feels the same as he always has, "except that it is rather harder now." She asks why, and he replies, "Because you be richer than you were at that time." She tells him she has made nearly all the money over to the baby, and has just enough to live on. Diggory answers, "I am rather glad of that, for it makes it easier for us to be friendly."

Comment

We feel sure now that Diggory Venn's dogged persistence is to be rewarded. A delightful bit here tells how tiny Eustacia is learning to walk. She is "now of the age when it is a matter of doubt with such characters whether they are intended to walk through the world on their hands or on their feet; so that they get into painful complications by trying both." Thomasin liked to give little Eustacia her airing and practice "on the green turf and shepherd's thyme, which formed a soft mat to fall headlong upon."

CHAPTER 3: THE SERIOUS DISCOURSE OF CLYM WITH HIS COUSIN

Clym has been "pondering on his duty to his cousin." He knows his mother wanted him and Thomasin to marry. Perhaps he ought to marry her. But he feels drained of all such feeling, and thinks he would be a poor husband. He has decided to be "an itinerant preacher." One evening he comes downstairs and finds Thomasin in the garden. He intends to ask her advice; but she asks first: as her "sort of guardian" does he approve of her marrying Mr. Venn? At first he is quite against it. His mother disapproved. Finally he decides she disapproved only because Diggory was a reddleman. Now that he has given up the trade, Clym feels his mother would bless the marriage. Soon after this talk, Humphrey tells Clym that Diggory and Thomasin are seeing a lot of each other. "You could get her away from him now, 'tis my belief, if you were only to set about it." Clym answers: "How can I have the conscience to marry after having driven two women to their deaths? ... After my experience I should consider it too much of a **burlesque** to go to church and take a wife.... I am going to keep a night-school; and I am going to turn preacher." A few days later, Thomasin tells Clym that she and Diggory are to be married "on the twenty-fifth of next month, if you don't object."

Comment

Hardy puts some wry philosophy into this chapter, while Clym is trying to decide what to do. "It is an unfortunate fact that any particular whim of parents which might have been dispersed by half an hour's conversation during their lives, becomes sublimated by their deaths into a fiat [order] most absolute, with such results to conscientious children as those parents, had they lived, would have been the first to decry." Thus, Clym can almost persuade himself that his mother wants him to marry Thomasin. His great disinclination for this, however, is stronger than her possible persuasion. He believes she could not wish the marriage now.

CHAPTER 4: CHEERFULNESS AGAIN ASSERTS ITSELF AT BLOOMS-END AND CLYM FINDS HIS VOCATION

On the day of the wedding, sounds of great activity come from Timothy Fairway's house. The men have gathered there to make a feather bed as a present for the newly-weds. As they talk and work, Grandfer Cantle hums away at a song he plans to sing to the newly married pair this evening. When they break off work to sit down to lunch, they hear wheels arriving. Here are Venn and Mrs. Venn, Yeobright, and a relative of Venn's. The men rush out and shout "Hurrah!" after the carriage.

There is merry-making at Clym's house that evening. Clym wanders about outside, glancing in at the window, and listening to the music. Charley comes walking by and stops to talk with him. Clym speaks of Charley's goodness to Eustacia, and Charley summons up courage to say, "I wish, Mr. Yeobright, you could give me something to keep that once belonged to her - if you don't mind." Clym leads him up to his back room, and, "taking out a sheet of tissue-paper unfolded from it two or three ... locks of raven hair." He selects one and gives it to Charley, who is tearfully grateful: "O, Mr. Clym, how good you are to me!" Clym walks a little way on the heath with Charley. When he returns, he finds Diggory and Thomasin ready to depart with little Eustacia and the nurse. They bid him a loving farewell. He goes into the now empty house and sits opposite his mother's old chair, remembering.

The next Sunday on Rainbarrow the villagers gather again, this time to hear Clym Yeobright preach the first of a series of "Sermons on the Mount," which he promises to deliver each Sunday afternoon "as long as the fine weather" lasts.

Comment

The making of a mattress of feathers, or a "feather bed" is described here in detail. The men in shirt-sleeves are gathered at Timothy Fairway's house. "Across the stout oak table ... was thrown a mass of striped linen which Grandfer Cantle held down on one side and Humphrey on the other, while Fairway rubbed its surface with a yellow lump" of beeswax. Waxing the tick will keep the feathers from sticking to the cloth. "When the bed was in proper trim, Fairway and Christian brought forward vast paper bags, stuffed to the full, but light as balloons.... As bag after bag was emptied, airy tufts of down and feathers floated about the room...." Christian Cantle missed the tick with one bag and "the atmosphere of the room became dense with gigantic flakes" descending "like a windless snowstorm." In all, seventy pounds of feathers are stuffed and sewed into the completed bedtick.

Hardy tidily closes his novel with parallels to its beginning. Grandfer Cantle rehearses a song to sing to Thomasin and her new husband, as he did at that other bonfire long ago, when the men made plans to serenade Thomasin and her husband at the inn. Rainbarrow, a pervasive presence, swarming with people in the early chapters, now swarms again for another gathering - the audience for Clym Yeobright's sermon.

Summary: Book Sixth is anticlimax. The novel was first published in installments, and Hardy's readers demanded a sequel - they wanted to know what became of the survivors, and especially that Diggory Venn was rewarded in his devotion to Thomasin. Thomasin must marry her faithful lover. Clym may be left alone, but he must be free to pursue his dearest ambitions.

1. Clym invites Thomasin to move to Blooms-End. Diggory Venn comes calling.

2. Thomasin and Diggory have a talk that Diggory says "makes it easier for us to be friendly.

3. Thomasin asks Clym's approval of her marriage to Diggory Venn. After some pondering, he gives it.

4. Thomasin and Diggory Venn are married. They leave Clym Yeobright to live alone in his old home, and to solace his soul with teaching and preaching. Hardy completes the novel's cycle this time with the final Rainbarrow scene. Once more, as in the opening scene of the novel, Rainbarrow is aswarm with heath folk, gathered this time to hear Clym preach.

THE RETURN OF THE NATIVE

EGDON HEATH

It is quite generally agreed that the heath is as strong a character as any in the novel-probably the strongest. It is the unique force that touches and molds all lives. The whole novel is played on Egdon Heath as on a stage, and the heath, in its turn, plays upon all the characters, molding their lives by its pervasive influence. H. M. Tomlinson in his essay in *The Saturday Review Gallery* voices this sentiment: "... It may still be true that the earth and the sky and the force we call life transcend in their mystery any character, however heroic or pitiable. The earth itself is the oldest, of characters; it was here when the earliest of us arrived... if you read again the first chapter of *The Return of the Native* ... then the shadow of Something which is greater than mortal life begins to fall upon your reading."

Hardy, the naturalist, enjoys writing of the heath. He writes of its sights: the purple bells of heather, the yellow gorse, the looming barrows, the heath croppers, the snakes, the flint knives and arrowheads of antiquity, the winding paths. He writes of its sounds: "the baritone buzz of a holly tree"; "the intermittent husky notes of the male grasshoppers"; the "worn whisper" of the wind through "the mummied heath-bells of the past Summer"; the sound of the fir-clump in the stirring air; the breeze through the furze-bushes; the roaring of the weir in the storm. Hardy writes of "the intonation of a pollard thorn a little way to windward, the breezes filtering through its unyielding twigs as through a strainer. It was as if the night sang dirges with clenched teeth." He writes of the insects of the heath: "among fallen apples on the ground beneath were wasps rolling drunk with the juice, or creeping about the little caves in each fruit which they had eaten out before stupefied by its sweetness." There were "little brown butterflies" and "a colony of ants [which] had established a thoroughfare ... where they toiled a never-ending and heavy-laden throng." He writes of the birds of the heath: "a heron ... had come dripping wet from some pool in the valleys and as he flew the edges and lining of his wings, his thighs, and his breast were so caught by the bright sunbeams that he appeared as if formed of burnished silver." Only a keen observer and an ardent lover of nature could think these thoughts, and only a Thomas Hardy could find the words to write them in so vivid a style.

EUSTACIA VYE

A black-haired, white-faced beauty, Eustacia has been described by Hardy as "Queen of the Night." Actually, she is a lonely, city-loving girl doomed to life on the heath. Self-pitying, she is always over-dramatizing her lot. She has the quick temper which goes with a too proud spirit. She has illusions of grandeur. At nineteen, she is driven by her passionate nature to take up with whatever man she can find. No man can resist her "flame-like" spirit. Too proud, she cannot lower herself to marry or run away with Wildeve, the man who could have given her the glitter of Parisian life. She chooses to marry Clym, who has turned his back on the artificial glamor of Paris. She expects to bend his will to hers, but finds herself at the last the wife of a furze-cutter. The heath people keep their distance from her. One mother believes her to be a witch and practices ancient superstitious rites against her. But one heath boy, hopelessly in love with her, treats her with deference and great kindness. The heath is to Eustacia a place to have secret meetings and moody walks. Her prayer is, "O deliver my heart from this fearful gloom and loneliness." She calls the heath "my cross, my misery ... (it) will be my death." It is her death. She drowns in the pool at the weir.

CLYM YEOBRIGHT

Clym's face is one that conveys "less the idea of so many years as its age as that of so much experience as its store." His habit of meditation makes people think his look odd rather than handsome. It is a look of natural cheerfulness overlaid with depression. He is a crusader who wants to help his kind. He values wisdom above affluence; ennoblement above repentance. His mother, disappointed at his decision to give up a flourishing diamond business to become a teacher, says, "I suppose you will be like your father; like him, you are getting weary of doing well." And Clym asks, "Mother, what is doing well?" She is too thoughtful a woman herself to have a ready answer.

The heath to Clym holds friendliness and geniality. Being no farmer, he is glad to see attempts at reclamation of the heathland retreat before ferns and furze-tufts. "If anyone knew the heath well, it was Clym. He was permeated with its scenes, with its substance, and with its odors.... Take all the varying hates felt by Eustacia Vye toward the heath, and translate them into loves, and you have the heart of Clym."

DAMON WILDEVE

Wildeve is a young man with "a profuse crop of hair impending over the top of his face ... and a neck ... smooth and round as a cylinder. The lower half of his figure" is light in build. He has a grace of movement that marks him for "a lady-killing career." He is a nervous, excitable man, capable of quick decisions made in anger or pique. Thomasin say, "he has an unfortunate manner and doesn't try to make people like him if they don't wish to do it of their own accord." He is a man of sentiment. Yearning for the difficult, weary of the easy; eager for the remote, losing interest when it is available; he will always find himself dissatisfied and restless. "The peculiarity of Wildeve was that, while at one time passionate, upbraiding, and resentful towards a woman, at another he would treat her with such unparalleled grace as to make previous neglect appear as no discourtesy, injury as no insult ... and the ruin of her honor as excess of chivalry." He is "a man of fair professional education, and one who has served his articles with a civil engineer." Some undisclosed misfortune has relegated him to the business of innkeeper. Of the heath he says to Eustacia, "I abhor it too ... How mournfully the wind blows round us.... God, how lonely it is! What are picturesque ravines and mists to us who see nothing else? Thomasin tells him he looks "at the heath as if it were somebody's goal."

THOMASIN YEOBRIGHT

Thomasin is a young girl with "a fair, sweet, and honest country face ... reposing in a nest of wavy chestnut hair." She has a hopeful spirit. She reminds "the beholder of the feathered creatures who lived around her home.... There was as much variety in her motions as in their flight. When she was musing she was a kestrel [small hawk], which hangs in the air by an invisible

97

motion of its wings. When she was in a high wind her light body was blown against trees and banks like a heron's When she was frightened she darted noiselessly like a kingfisher. When she was serene she skimmed like a swallow." Thomasin's nature is one that takes life as it comes, philosophically and happily. Her aunt calls her "a practical little woman." She has pluck, too, and self-respect: "Do I look like a lost woman? ... I wish all good women were as good as I!" is her reaction to the gossip about her having been jilted. She has her own kind of pride: "I belong to one man; nothing can alter that. And that man I must marry, for my pride's sake," She is not one to contrive. Others contrive for her so that she gets her desire. Diggory Venn contrives out of the desire to see her happy. Mrs. Yeobright contrives because she feels the dignity of the family must be upheld. Eustacia Vye contrives in order to eliminate her as a rival.

The heath to Thomasin is "a ridiculous old place" she has gotten accustomed to and couldn't be happy without. She thinks of it as "a nice wild place to walk in." She likes to take baby Eustacia to romp and roll on the soft green turf. "To her there were not, as to Eustacia Vye, demons in the air and malice in every bush and bough...." In a storm, "the drops which lashed her face were not scorpions but prosy rain. At this time it was in her view a windy, wet place, in which a person might experience much discomfort, lose the path without care, and possibly catch cold."

DIGGORY VENN

Venn is a handsome young man with keen blue eyes and a good figure. His clothes are of good cut and excellent quality. He as a well-to-do-air. When we first meet him, he is "completely red. One dye of that tincture covered his clothes, the cap upon his head, his boots, his face, and his hands." The color permeated him. "He was more decently born and brought up than the cattle-drovers ... but they merely nodded to him. His stock was more valuable than that of pedlars; but they ... passed his cart with eyes straight ahead. He was such an unnatural color to look at that the men of the roundabouts and waxwork shows seemed gentlemen beside him; but he considered them low company, and remained aloof.... His occupation tended to isolate him."

Diggory is traveling over the heath as a reddleman, a humble occupation for so personable a young man. We wonder why. He is in love with Thomasin Yeobright, and that young lady has refused his proposal of marriage. In his disappointment, he has turned from his prosperous dairy farm and roams the heath, living in his van. He contrives to be in the vicinity of Thomasin without bothering her. He is her self-appointed guardian angel. His single-minded purpose in life is to see that she is happy. Diggory Venn is a thread woven through the novel to trip up the transgressors at strategic moments. His shrewd maneuvers harass Eustacia and Damon Wildeve, and turn the tide against them. To Diggory, the heath is a familiar; a friendly place to live in; a congenial spirit, helpful to his purpose and plots.

MRS. YEOBRIGHT

Mrs. Yeobright is the proud, middle-aged mother of a successful son. Her husband, now dead, had been a farmer; "she herself was a curate's daughter, who had once dreamed of doing better things." She is a respected widow "of a standing which can only be expressed by the word genteel." It is a great blow to her to have her son, Clym, come home to live as a teacher, after he has been a successful money-maker in Paris. She is further crushed to have Clym marry "the hussy," Eustacia Vye. Mrs. Yeobright is a quick-tempered, self-pitying woman, who will, however, relent when appealed to in the right way. She possesses "two distinct moods... a gentle mood and an angry," and she can fly from one to the other "without the least warning." She is undemonstrative, yet she has a kind heart for those she cares for. Those she dislikes she treats with "grim friendliness." She expresses Hardy's philosophy in her words: "Cry about one thing in life, cry about all; one thread runs through the whole piece." The heath deals her a death-blow as she walks nearly ten miles over its parched, searingly hot paths on a scorching August day.

CAPTAIN VYE

Eustacia's grandfather is an absent-minded old gentleman. He has been a naval officer. He chose his spot on the health at Mistover, because, with a telescope, he could see the English Channel on fine days. He lets his granddaughter run wild on the heath. He chuckles at her schemes and admonishes her good-naturedly; he means well but does not know how to cope with her powerful character.

THE RUSTICS

Albert Guerard says that Hardy's rustic characters are compact personalities revealed by their motions, their words, their jokes, and their deficiencies. They take great pleasure in telling tales of their past escapades, but they have no present conflicts connected with the plot. Such a character is Grandfer Cantle. He uses a stick as a third leg, and dances and sings with zest, though they say of him, "There's a hole in thy poor bellows nowadays seemingly." He brags shamelessly about his adventures when he "went a soldier in the Bang-up Locals in the year four." He belittles his poor slowwitted son, saying, "Really all the soldiering and

THE RETURN OF THE NATIVE

smartness in the world in the father seems to count for nothing in forming the nater of the son. As far as that Chile Christian is concerned I might as well have stayed at home and seed nothing, like all the rest of ye here." He provides a comic relief with his jigs and boasting. Christi Cantle, his son, is all fears and timidity. He is depressed by his unmarriageable state. He is easily deceived and victimized. Charley is a rather pitiful fellow, with his unrequited love for Eustacia. He is also a likable fellow. In his small way, he is as solicitous for Eustacia's happiness as Diggory Venn is for Thomasin's. Timothy Fairway seems to be the leader among the heath folk. It is he who supervises the grappling for the well-bucket; he who does the village hair-cutting; he who takes charge at the gatherings. Susan Nunsuch, whose boy Johnny does chores for Eustacia, is a superstitious woman who uses magic to protect him from Eustacia's fancied witchery. She comes nearer to connection with the plot than most others. Sam, the turf-cutter, Humphrey, the furze cutter, and Olly Dowden, the besom-maker, round out the number of heath rustics. Guerard calls the country characters alive and vivid but not developed and buffeted by circumstances as are the main characters of the novel. They give a comic relief and serve to express earthy wisdom in their tales. Their reminiscences provide a strong connection with the past. They are not nineteenth century Dorset, but are drawn from Wessex's still living history. In other words, they are quaint people whose habits and talk have been untouched by modern progress.

THE RETURN OF THE NATIVE

USE OF WORDS

Thomas Hardy was a keen observer of nature and of people. As a little boy playing with the heath children, he quickly caught the country dialect; so much so that his parents would not allow him to use it at home. One element of his style is his use of this country dialect. He can recreate it so that the country folk in their conversations "ring true" to the Wessex past as colorful individuals and as heath people. The reader will notice that Hardy's main characters speak the ordinary English of educated people. lacks the sparkle of the dialect; it depends on the expressed thoughts of the individual to give it life. In other words, dialogue, to be arresting, may express interesting thoughts and schemes of dynamic individuals, or it may be a dialect full of odd words and homely sayings.

Hardy uses a completely different way with words for his descriptions and philosophizings. Here are words of many syllables, Biblical references, references to Greek mythology, long sentences; here is the poet enjoying the creation of word-pictures in rhythmic meter. Hardy loved nature - animals, flowers, trees, insects, birds, storms, the heath. When he writes of these, he chooses his words lovingly, with great sensitivity for the right turn of phrase or choice of word to describe a bird in flight, twilight on the heath, winds playing upon the heath as on an instrument. His nature passages take time to appreciate; slow thoughtful reading of them is rewarding.

In addition to these three ways of using words, Hardy also has his moments of straightforward narration to help plunge the action onward. Katherine Anne Porter, in *Modern Literary Criticism*, says of Hardy's style that his **episodes** may seem dull in the reading but one feels in retrospect that he has lived the episodes. As one reads, the action seems almost to disappear, but afterward in contemplation it all comes back in clear focus.

CHARACTERS

Hardy is at his best in creating women characters. He infuses them with a spirit individual to each. They reveal themselves through their conversations, as in the encounter of Mrs. Yeobright with Eustacia by the pool at Mistover. What they say gives them away for what they are. For example: Eustacia, goaded beyond endurance by Mrs. Yeobright, blurts out that she would have thought twice before marrying Clym if she had known that she would be doomed to life on the heath.

The men in the novel seem to be characterized more by their actions; for example, Diggory Venn's actions in thwarting Wildeve at every turn, including the gambling bout on the heath, make him seem puckish, a sort of wizard or magician, appearing and disappearing at precisely the right moment, but never saying many words. Albert Guerard says that Hardy's power to dramatize the feminine personality and temperament is extraordinary, but his interesting men are fewer than those found in almost any other important novel. Katherine Anne Porter says that those of his characters who are swayed by their emotions come to tragedy. He seems to be warning us that to follow the emotions blindly will lead to disaster. It is true that Thomasin, Diggory Venn, and Clym, the characters who have thought out their desires and planned for them, are the ones who find peace of mind, regardless of disappointments. Eustacia, Wildeve, and Mrs. Yeobright, the emotional ones, come to tragic ends.

THE SUBLIME

Many evaluations of Hardy's style include a discussion of his use of the Sublime. S. F. Johnson, in *Style in Prose Fiction*, has an essay called "Hardy and Burke's 'Sublime.'" Johnson presents the Sublime as the deepest emotion which the mind can feel. He compares it to a diamond with many facets. Hardy uses all seven of Burke's component parts of the Sublime, and adds, according to Johnson, two of his own: Terror, Obscurity, Power (God or Fate), Privation (or Solitude), Vastness (Infinity), Magnificence, Feeling (especially, bodily pain), and Hardy's Grotesque (Ugliness) and Tragedy.

All these qualities of the Sublime appear in the scene on Rainbarrow where Eustacia crouches in the storm, before going down the heath to throw herself into Shadwater Weir pool. Eustacia is terrified at the outlook before her as it suddenly bursts upon her thought that she has no money; she feels obscure and helpless against Fate; she feels deprived of her birthright: "How I have tried and tried to be a splendid woman and how destiny is against me!" The Vastness of the world overwhelms her, making her feel completely unable to cope with any problem; she cries out in terrible pain: "O how hard it is of Heaven to devise such tortures for me."

Hers is a great tragedy of the soul. "Never was harmony more perfect than that between the chaos of her mind and the chaos of the world without." There is a magnificence in the power of the storm-tossed heath and the storm-tossed soul. There is certain ugliness in her bitter spirit of revolt against "this ill-conceived world." The moment is the culmination of all Eustacia's frustrated hopes, fears, joys, passions - a great burst of the Tragedy of the Sublime.

Hardy was a great story-teller, blessed with an uninhibited imagination. He was a master architect of atmosphere: a sense of the aura pervading the heath pervades the whole novel. He builds depth on depth of images in sounds, sights, scents, and rhythms of the heath. He had a great sympathy for ordinary human beings in their battle against the circumstances and the environment of their lives. He makes us feel that same sympathy, even while we may be exasperated with the person involved; therein lies his genius. Katherine Anne Porter sums this up when she says that tragedy of the best and highest sort deals with worthy people who are surrounded by the inevitable against which they are powerless. Hardy's characters suffer simply because they are alive.

Hardy was a deep thinker. He spent long hours pondering over the principle of life itself: why we are here, what we can do with ourselves, what forces are with us, what forces are against us, how we influence others, how others influence us, and how nature works for one person and against another. In particular he studied the workings of "fate" (heredity and environment) especially upon women. He saw women as irresponsible, untrustworthy, and alluring. He created women who appeal to men by their very waywardness. He seemed to regard women with sympathy but also with reserve, as if he found them fascinating but fearsome.

For nature his feeling is more unreserved and intimate. The sky, the earth, the season changes, the growing things all have a compelling charm for him that men and women with all their struggles and passions cannot quite approach. What fun and enjoyment Hardy finds in life comes from his spectator contemplation of the lowly peasants and animals whose quaint, archaic ways always amuse him. He appreciates their earthy wisdom.

In The Return of the Native, particular stress is given to the revitalizing power of rural life, for example Clym's return to the heath and its values for him. Hardy, in all his novels, is apparently preoccupied with the problems of marriage. *In The Return of the Native* he probes the anxieties of the faithful wife (Thomasin) with the philandering husband (Wildeve) and those of the restless wife (Eustacia) with the faithful husband (Clym).

Hardy has himself said that "the business of the poet and novelist is to show the sorriness underlying the grandest things, and the grandeur underlying the sorriest things." This is perhaps the basic characteristic of his art - that he sees these things and can communicate them to us, his readers.

THE RETURN OF THE NATIVE

· ·

Question: Describe in detail all the gambling scenes in *The Return of the Native*. Explain the importance of each.

Answer: The first scene is the raffle at the Inn. Christian Cantle is the hero of this piece. He has Mrs. Yeobright's guineas in his boots and some silver in his pocket. He is on his way to the wedding celebration at Mistover for the purpose of delivering the guineas to Clym and Thomasin. He meets neighbors who are going to the raffle. They persuade him that "no black art" is involved, and that he must come along to see the fun. Once there, he is persuaded to throw in his shilling with the rest. When he shakes the dice, he throws a pair-royal and wins the gown-piece. This scene is important because Christian is hereby convinced that he has a power in him over the dice. It is a brand new thought to the simple, timid man; it makes him for the first time feel powerful. He confides in Wildeve that he could use this power to do good to "a near relation of yours." Wildeve's curiosity is aroused and his gambling spirit touched. He knows he can get the best of Christian in a dice game, and he guesses Christian has money for Thomasin-money which Mrs. Yeobright refused to trust to him. He resolves to get even with Mrs. Yeobright by winning the money and scornfully handing it to Thomasin in Mrs. Yeobright's presence. When Christian asks if he can take the dice that carry his luck inside them, Wildeve is only too happy to give them to him. He offers to walk to Mistover in the dusk with Christian. He will fleece the gullible Christian on the way.

And so he does. As they walk across the heath in the warm night, Wildeve gets Christian to admit he has money for Thomasin and that what is wife's is husband's. Then Wildeve, feigning weariness, asks that they sit down for a bit. Christian puts the lantern on the ground and rattles the dice in his pocket, calling them "magical machines." Wildeve urges Christian on in his belief that he has power over the dice, saying that he himself is not so lucky. He tells Christian one story after another of men who have been lucky in gambling. He ends with a story of a man in America who lost his last dollar, his watch, his umbrella, his hat, his coat - and was about to take off his breeches, when a man gave him a coin for his pluck. With this he "won back his coat, won back his hat, won back his umbrella, his watch, his money, and went out of the door a rich man." Christian is, of course, now so excited that he must play. Wildeve, of course, wins all Christian's money, then lets him play with Mrs. Yeobright's guineas and wins those. Only after Christian has lost all does he reveal that half the guineas are Clym's. Wildeve is delighted at another chance to have revenge on Mrs. Yeobright. He plans to give Clym's share to Eustacia.

But, no sooner has Christian left to go unhappily home, than Diggory Venn appears out of the bushes. He was at the inn raffle, and, understanding Wildeve's intent to victimize Christian, followed the pair and listened in on the game. Now he challenges Wildeve, and he, of course, wins back all the money- at each throw mocking Wildeve with "won back his coat" - "won back his hat" - "won back his watch, his money, and went out the door a rich man." Wildeve is now beside himself with rage and lust for gambling. The heath-croppers have gathered around to watch. Wildeve in a frenzy throws away the dice. They hunt and find one. The game proceeds with only one. A moth flies in and puts out the lantern. They have no matches. Wildeve is so wild to play, he gathers thirteen glowworms, and arranges them in a circle on a stone so they can go on playing. Diggory wins again and again till Wildeve has no money to play.

Here is the faithful guardian foiling the schemer who has just victimized the "simpleton." Diggory Venn, always watchful for Thomasin's interests, wins again for her. Here we have Hardy's reason winning out over blind instinct. Venn has plotted and carried his scheme through. Wildeve merely "played the thing by ear," following his fancy of the moment. Diggory Venn, however, unknowingly widens the breach between Clym and his mother by his mistaken idea that the guineas are all for Thomasin and giving them all to her.

Question: Describe what the heath means to Eustacia, to Clym, to Thomasin, to Wildeve, and to Diggory Venn.

Answer: To Eustacia, the heath is a prison, gloomy and lonely. She believes it is "her cross, her misery" and that it will be her death. To her there are "demons in the air" and "malice in every bush." However, she seems to enjoy taking long walks on the heath. Her dramatic nature thrills to clandestine meetings with Wildeve under Rainbarrow. She likes the drama of the bonfire signal. One thinks that, possibly, if she would let herself go, would relax into the drama of the heath, she might grow to feel at one with its moods. She refuses to do this; herein is her tragedy.

To Clym, the heath is a friend. He gathers refreshment and inspiration from long walks on the heath. When he loses his eyesight for reading, he finds solace on the heath in the humble work of furze-cutting. The heath gives him happiness in misfortune. Clym yields his nature to the nature of the heath.

To Thomasin, the heath is a "ridiculous old place"; a nice wild place to walk in; a place where her baby can romp on the soft green turf. She is very matter-of-fact about it. It is a place she is used to and could not be happy without. Being out on the heath in a storm does not mean demons and malice to Thomasin, it means possibly catching a cold.

To Wildeve, the heath is lonely, mournful, "a dismal gaol." He seems, however, to enjoy dodging around the heath for chance meetings with Eustacia. He, too, thrills to the drama of signals. He sends a moth to fly around the lamp when he wants to signal to Eustacia for a rendezvous. One might feel about him, as about Eustacia, that he could meet the turbulence of the heath with his own turbulent nature, if he wished to try. This is Hardy's message: that those who buck against nature lose out.

To Diggory Venn, the heath is a matter-of-fact place. He hardly thinks of it; he lives in it. He uses the heath ponies to help in his work. He finds the heath a roomy place where he can be near to help Thomasin without bothering her. He uses the heath as a friend to help further his schemes. For example, he took advantage of the piled up turves to camouflage himself so that he might move nearer to eavesdrop on Wildeve and Eustacia. Diggory Venn and the heath are at one with each other.

Question: Tell in detail how Diggory Venn thwarts Damon Wildeve time after time.

Answer: Besides outwitting Wildeve in the gambling on the heath Venn gets the better of him in several ways. He connives with Eustacia, for instance, to get Wildeve to marry Thomasin. First he tries flattery, saying she has power over Wildeve and can influence him to marry Thomasin. When this does not work, he flatters her about her "comeliness." He appeals to her vanity, saying any man will comply with her wishes. She says she does not particularly want to do anything for Thomasin, and she intimates that she does not know Wildeve, anyhow. He confronts her with the truth: "the woman that stands between Wildeve and Thomasin is yourself." She becomes flustered, and he uses her discomfiture to play his last card. He shrewdly offers to get her away from the heath. He tells her she is too good for such life. He knows a widow in Budmouth who wants a companion, and he will take Eustacia to her. Eustacia will not yield. Diggory Venn gets his way, at a later date, however. When Eustacia has decided she wants Thomasin to marry Wildeve so she herself will have no rival for Clym's affections, Diggory is the one to whom she gives her note of refusal, to be delivered to Wildeve. When Diggory delivers this message, he also reveals his own interest in Thomasin. The combination of circumstances-frustration in his plans for marrying Eustacia, the blow to his pride, the realization that Thomasin is sought by another sends Wildeve immediately down the heath to set the date for marriage with Thomasin.

After Eustacia and Thomasin are married, Diggory Venn has now to protect Thomasin's happiness by thwarting Wildeve's attempts to meet with Eustacia. He makes a grass trap to trip him up. He spoils his plan to meet Eustacia by rapping loudly on the door and disappearing. He shoots at Wildeve from the bushes. He goes to Mrs. Yeobright to urge her to go to see Clym and Eustacia and make friends with them, hoping to make

Clym's marriage more successful and Eustacia less eager to meet Wildeve. Finally, he goes with Thomasin to try to prevent the elopement of Wildeve and Eustacia.

Question: Compare Eustacia's three lovers.

Answer: Wildeve is a lady's man who cannot resist chasing after a pretty girl. He and Eustacia are alike in giving rein to impulsive passions and tempers. They torture each other with their come-hithers and their thrusting-away. Wildeve sympathizes with Eustacia's longing for glamor and glitter in her life. He tries to get her away. He impulsively jumps to save her from drowning, drowning himself in the attempt. Although he seems to be cast in the role of a philanderer, we can often see good impulses in his thoughts and deeds. Actually, he is human, with good and bad mixed up in him.

Clym is an earnest, thoughtful young man, anxious to do good in the world. He falls under the spell of Eustacia's passionate nature and must marry her. He mistakenly believes she will help him in his teaching. She mistakenly believes he will take her to Paris. Both are doomed to disappointment in each other. His love survives the shock, but coincidental circumstances intervene to deprive him of reconciliation. (His letter is never delivered to Eustacia.) When he goes to save Eustacia from drowning, he acts more rationally than Wildeve, and survives to live on in a solitary life with his memories of his love. He follows his plan of becoming a teacher and a preacher, but Hardy makes us feel that the heath folk will not be particularly receptive to new ideas and enrichment of their mental lives. As one says: "'Tis good-hearted of the young man, but, for my part, I think he had better mind his business."

Charley is a simple country boy who worships Eustacia. He bargains to held her hand for fifteen minutes, and doesn't want to "use it all up at once." When Eustacia returns, cast out, to her grandfather's house, Charley treats her with the utmost kindness and reverence. He gets food for her, makes her comfortable; and later brings all sorts of tokens from the heath to try to amuse her. He protects her from shooting herself. After her death, he asks Clym for something which belonged to her. Clym gives him a lock of Eustacia's hair, for which Charley is fervently grateful.

Question: One of the charms of Hardy's narrative, as well as a means of providing atmosphere, is his treatment of country customs. Enumerate as many of these customs as you can and describe them.

Answer:

1. The Guy Fawkes Day bonfire celebration.

2. The custom of storing apples in beds of fern.

3. The Christmas Mummers' Play.

4. Braiding a woman's hair in different numbers of strands.

5. The village Sunday hair-cutting for the men.

6. Superstition of piercing with a needle to exorcize a devil.

7. Grappling for a well-bucket.

8. The opening of a barrow.

9. The raffle at the inn.

10. A village Gipsying.

11. Superstition of burning a wax effigy to cast out a devil.

12. The village Maypoling.

13. Waxing a bedtick and making a feather bed.

BIBLIOGRAPHY

In choosing a copy of *The Return of the Native* for use in studying the novel, editions with notes by scholars in the field are particularly valuable. Paperbound editions of this type are:

Hardy, Thomas, *The Return of the Native*:

J. W. Cunliffe, editor. Scribner.

Afterword by Albert Guerard. Washington Square Press.

Albert Guerard, Jr., editor. Holt.

Afterword by Horace Gregory, Signet Classics.

Introduction by Irving Howe. Collier.

GENERAL: LIFE AND WORKS OF THOMAS HARDY

Blunden, Edmund, *Thomas Hardy*, New York: St. Martin's, 1941.

Brennecke, Ernest, Jr., *The Life of Thomas Hardy*, New York: Greenberg, Publisher, Inc., 1925.

Hardy, Florence Emily, *The Life of Thomas Hardy*, New York: St. Martin's Press, 1962.

Scott-James, R. A., *Thomas Hardy*, New York: London House, 1951.

Weber, Carl J., *Hardy of Wessex, His Life and Literary Career*, Hamden, Conn.: Shoe String, 1962.

Wing, George, *Thomas Hardy*, New York: Grove (Evergreen Pilot, EP 22), 1963.

ESSAYS ON LIFE AND WORKS

Blunden, E. C., *Edmund Blunden*, New York: Horizon Press, 1961. "Notes on Visits to Thomas Hardy," pp. 272–278.

Ford, Ford Madox, *Portraits from Life*, Chapter VI, "Thomas Hardy," Boston: Houghton Mifflin, 1937, pp. 90–106.

Beatty, Jerome, Jr. ed. *The Saturday Review Gallery*, New York: Simon and Schuster, 1959.

Hardy at Max Gate," by H. M. Tomlinson, pp. 141–148.

BOOKS ON HARDY'S THEMES AND LITERARY TECHNIQUES

Beach, Joseph W., *The Technique of Thomas Hardy*, New York: Russell, 1961.

Duffin, Henry C., *Thomas Hardy - A Study of the Wessex Novels, the Poems, and the Dynasts*, New York: Barnes and Noble, 1962.

Grimsditch, Herbert B., *Character and Environment in the Novels of Thomas Hardy*, New York: Russell, 1962.

Guerard, Albert J., ed., *Hardy: A Collection of Critical Essays*, Englewood Cliffs, N. J.: Prentice-Hall, 1963.

Guerard, Albert J., *Thomas Hardy - The Novels and Stories*, Cambridge, Mass.: Harvard Univ. Press, 1949.

Rutland, William, *Thomas Hardy: A Study of His Writings and Their Background*, New York: Russell, 1962.

Webster, Harvey Curtis, *On a Darkling Plain*, Chicago: University of Chicago Press, 1947.

ESSAYS ON HARDY'S THEMES AND LITERARY TECHNIQUES

Howe, Irving, ed., *Modern Literary Criticism - An Anthology*, Boston: Beacon Press, 1958. "On a Criticism of Thomas Hardy," by Katherine Anne Porter, pp. 299–309.

Martin, Harold C., Ed., *Style in Prose Fiction*, New York: Columbia Univ. Press, 1959. "Hardy and Burke's 'Sublime'," by S. F. Johnson, pp. 55–86.

Stallman, R. W., *The Houses That James Built*, East Lansing: Michigan State Univ. Press, 1961. "Hardy's Hour-glass Novel," pp. 53–63. [Specifically about *The Return of the Native*.]

Woolf, V. S., *The Second Common Reader*, New York: Harcourt Brace, 1932. "The Novels of Thomas Hardy," pp. 266–280.

ON CONTENT OF HARDY'S NOVELS

Firor, Ruth A., *Folkways in Thomas Hardy*, (paperbound, New York: Barnes, A. S., 1962).

Saxelby, F. O., *Thomas Hardy Dictionary*, New York: Humanities, n.d.

MAGAZINE ARTICLES

Cecil, R., "Twice Hardy; Review of Hardy the Novelist," *Saturday Review*, Sept. 28, 1946.

Tomlinson, H. M., "Thomas Hardy Country," *Holiday*, Nov. '53, pp. 54–55.

Weber, C. J., "Hardy: a Wessex Seesaw," *Saturday Review*, Jan. 6, 1951, pp. 24–25.

Weber, C. J., "Hardk in America," *Saturday Review*, Sept. 28, 1946, p. 10.

SUGGESTED TOPICS FOR FURTHER RESEARCH

1. Explain how the novel does or does not seem true to life.

2. Point out how Hardy's use of nature enriches the novel and forms an important background for the action.

3. Compare descriptions of English heath country in travel books with heath country in Hardy's novels.

4. Analyze the novel from the point of view of "Gothic" techniques, such as magic, nature, and gloom.

5. Defend Clym Yeobright, Diggory Venn, and Damon Wildeve as possible heroes of *The Return of the Native*, and explain why Hardy considered Clym the hero.

6. Discuss melodrama as it appears in the novel.

7. After reading all three, explain the sense in which *The Return of the Native*, *Tess of the D'urbervilles*, and *Jude the Obscure* may each be considered the greatest of Hardy's novels, and defend your own opinion.

8. Determine the role of Fate (destiny, coincidence) in the lives of each of the characters in the novel.

9. Examine Hardy's poetry. Does it have the same basic **themes** as *The Return of the Native*?

10. What evidences are there in the novel of Hardy's architectural experience and interest?

11. Point out examples in the novel where the weather conditions parallel the characters' moods.

12. Make an analysis of the social hierarchy in the novel.

13. Discuss the novel in terms of exterior and interior conflicts of the characters.

14. Compare the heath in *Jane Eyre* to the heath in *The Return of the Native*.

15. Discuss folkways or customs of the heath people.

16. Study the topography of the "Wessex" countryside. Is Hardy realistic as he pictures it in the novel?

17. What makes this an English novel rather than a French or an American novel?

18. Make a detailed discussion of the varieties of settings in the novel.

19. Discuss the psychological conflicts in the main characters.

20. Discuss the novel from the point of view of a naturalist.

GLOSSARY

Adam: The first man. (Biblical.)

Aegean: Sea between Greece and Asia Minor.

Aeneas: A Trojan, hero of Virgil's *Aeneid*.

Aeschylus: Greek writer of tragedies.

Ahasuerus: A Jew condemned to wander about the world till Christ's Second Coming.

Albertus Magnus: Bavarian philosopher and theologian of the Dominican order, called the Universal Doctor.

Alcinous: Prosperous king of Phaeacia.

Alexander: King of Macedonia.

Alps: Mountain system in Europe.

Amerigo Vespucci: Italian navigator after whom America is named.

Antediluvian: Of the time before the Flood. (Biblical.)

Arab: A Bedouin, or wanderer.

Archipelago: A sea with many islands.

Artemis: Goddess of the moon. (Greek mythology.)

Athalie: A play by the French dramatist, Racine.

Athena: Goddess of wisdom. (Greek mythology.)

Atlantean: Of Atlas, the huge man who carried the world on his shoulders. (Greek legend.) Babylon: Ancient city on the Euphrates River. (Biblical.)

Baden: State in Germany.

Balaam: Prophet hired to curse Israelites; when he beat his donkey, the animal rebuked him. (Biblical.)

Begum: Sheridan's Begum Speech made in Parliament (lasted six hours).

Belshazzar: The last king of Babylon. (Biblical.)

Bois: Park on the outskirts of Paris.

Buonaparte: Napoleon Bonaparte, the French general.

Bustard: A heavy, long-legged game bird.

Caesar: Roman statesman and general.

Cain: Oldest son of Adam and Eve; killed his brother Abel. (Biblical.)

Candaules: Legendary king of Lydia, a part of Asia Minor.

Carpe diem: Make the most of today (literally, seize the day).

Carthaginian: Of Carthage, a state in northern Africa.

Castle of Indolence: A long poem by Thomson.

Celts: An ancient people in central and western Europe.

Christendom: Parts of the world where the Christian faith is professed.

Cima-recta: An S-shaped curve.

Cimmerian Land: A region of perpetual mist and darkness.

Cleopatra: A queen of Egypt; Anthony (Roman general) and Cleopatra were two famous lovers of history.

Clive: Robert Clive, a great military leader and governor of Bengal.

Corfiote: From the Greek island of Corfu.

Coup-de-Jarnac: An unforeseen and decisive stroke.

Courser: A hawk.

Cretan Labyrinth: A maze constructed for the king of Crete.

David: Second king of Israel. (Biblical.)

Delphian: Oracular, prophetic (from Delphic oracle).

De Vere: Arthur De Vere, son of the Earl of Leicester.

Doomsday Book: Record of William I's great survey of lands of England made in 1608.

Druidical: Prophetic. Druids were Celtic priests or soothsayers.

Dureresque: Durer was a German painter and wood engraver.

Endor: Witch of Endor was a woman with a familiar spirit, asked by Saul to call up Samuel to prophesy. (Biblical.)

Etna: Mountain in Sicily, volcanic.

Exmoor: A moorland region in Somersetshire and Devonshire, England.

Florentine: Dante, the Italian poet.

Fontainebleau: Site of a palace of former kings of France.

Galloway: Horse of small, strong breed from southwest Scotland.

Gay: John Gay, composer of operas and plays.

Gethsemane: Garden where Jesus was arrested. (Biblical.)

Greaves of brass: Warrior's shin armor.

Heidelberg: University town in Baden, Germany.

Hades: Home of the dead. (Greek mythology.)

Heloise: Heloise and Abelard, French philosopher, are famous lovers of history.

Hera: Queen of the gods. (Greek mythology.)

Homer: Great Greek poet.

Hussars: European military horsemen.

Hypochondriasis: Abnormal anxiety over one's health.

Ikenild Street: The Roman highway.

Ishmaelitish: Outcast, one at war with society.

Ithuriel: An angel in Milton's *Paradise Lost*.

Jacob: Father of the founders of twelve tribes of Israel. (Biblical.)

Jarnac: Famous duelist (French).

John the Baptist: Forerunner and baptizer of Jesus. (Biblical.)

Judas Iscariot: Betrayer of Jesus. (Biblical.)

Keats: English poet.

Lammas-tide: August first, harvest festival.

Laura: Petrarch's beloved.

Leland: Earliest of modern English students of antiquity.

Limbo: A region bordering upon Hell, in some Christian theologies.

Louvre: Art museum in Paris.

Lydia Languish: Heroine of Sheridan's *The Rivals*, a play.

Maenades: Frenzied women. (Greek mythology.)

Marsh-harriers: Swift running, African birds.

Mary Stuart: Queen of Scotland.

Mephistophelian: Devilish, fiendish. (Mephistopheles was the name of the devil in Goethe's *Faust*.)

Moslem: A follower of Mohammed.

Napoleon: French general.

Nebo: Mountain from which Moses saw the Promised Land. (Biblical.)

Nebuchadnezzar: King of Babylon. (Biblical.)

North: Frederick North, prime minister of England.

Oedipus: King of Thebes. (Greek legend.)

Ogee: An S-shaped curve.

Olympus: High mountain in Greece called the home of the gods. (Greek mythology.)

Paul: St. Paul, a Jew of Tarsus, apostle of Christianity. (Biblical.)

Petrarch: Italian poet, lover of Laura.

Perugino: Italian painter.

Phaeacia: A land in Homer's *Odyssey*.

Pheidias: A famous Athenian maker of statues.

Philistines: Non-semitic peoples warring against the Israelites.

Pis aller: Last resort.

Plato: Greek philosopher.

Polaris: The North Star.

Polly Peachum: Heroine of Gay's *Beggar's Opera*.

Pontius Pilate: Roman governor of Judea. (Biblical.)

Promethean: Courageous, Prometheus was a Titan who stole fire from heaven for use of mankind. (Greek mythology.)

Pyracanth: Evergreen thorny shrub.

Queen of Love: Venus or Aphrodite. (Roman or Greek mythology.)

Raffaelle: Raphael, the Italian painter.

Rasselas: Romance by Samuel Johnson.

Rembrandt: Dutch painter.

Rogers: Samuel Rogers, English poet.

Rousseau: French philosopher.

Sappho: A woman poet of ancient Greece.

Saracen: A Moslem opposed to the Crusaders.

Saul: First king of Israel. (Biblical.)

Saxons: An ancient Germanic people who invaded England.

Scheherazade: Teller of tales who saved her life by keeping the Sultan interested.

Scheveningen: Coastal town in the Netherlands.

Scyllaeo-Charybdean: Between two evils. Scylla was a dangerous rock; Charybdis was a dangerous whirlpool.

Sennacherib: King of Assyria. (Biblical.)

Sheridan: Richard Brinsley Sheridan, the playwright, who made a famous six-hour speech in Parliament.

Siddons: Mrs. Sarah Siddons, and English actress.

Sisera: A military leader. (Biblical.)

Skimmity-riding: Skimmington, a ludicrous procession with figures carried on a pole, exposing and ridiculing marital quarrels.

Socrates: The Athenian philosopher.

Schleswig: A former duchy of Denmark.

Sphinx: An Egyptian statue having the body of a lion and the head of a man.

Strafford: Sir Thomas Strafford, nicknamed Black Tom Tyrant.

Sumner: Charles Sumner, American statesman and abolitionist.

Tantalus: Son of Zeus, doomed to stand in water which always receded when he tried to drink. (Greek mythology.)

Tartarean: Infernal, hellish. Tartarus was name for Hell. (Greek mythology.)

Teutonic: German.

Thor: God of thunder. (Norse or Scandinavian mythology.)

Thule: A far away, unknown region.

Titanic: Gigantic. Titan was a gigantic man of superhuman strength. (Greek mythology.)

Tuileries: Royal palace in Paris.

Tussaud: Madame Tussaud's waxworks in London.

Ulysses: Greek chief ant king of Ithaca. (Greek legend.)

Vale of Tempe: A beautiful valley between Mounts Olympus and Ossa, in Thessaly, Greece.

Versailles: Site of palace built by Louis XIV.

Via Iceniana: The Roman highway.

Vicinal way: Local road, not a highway.

West: Benjamin West, American painter in England.

William the Conqueror: Norman Duke who invaded England, 1066.

Woden: The chief Germanic god. (Teutonic mythology.)

Zenobia: An ambitious woman who invaded Asia Minor and Egypt.